The Microsoft® Platform Ahead

David S. Platt

PUBLISHED BY
Microsoft Press
A Division of Microsoft Corporation
One Microsoft Way
Redmond, Washington 98052-6399

Library of Congress Cataloging-in-Publication Data pending.

Printed and bound in the United States of America.

1 2 3 4 5 6 7 8 9   QWE   8 7 6 5 4

Appendix A contains a chapter from *Introducing Microsoft SQL Server 2005 for Developers* (Microsoft Press, 2005). Copyright © 2004 by Peter DeBetta.

Distributed in Canada by H.B. Fenn and Company Ltd.

A CIP catologue record for this book is available from the British Library.

Microsoft Press books are available through booksellers and distributors worldwide. For further information about international editions, contact your local Microsoft Corporation office or contact Microsoft Press International directly at fax (425) 936-7329. Visit our Web site at www.microsoft.com/learning/books. Send comments to *mspinput@microsoft.com*.

Acquisitions Editor: Ben Ryan
Project Editor: Karen Szall
Indexer: Patricia Masserman

Body Part No. X10-58060

To my family

Table of Contents

Preface

It's been three years since I first wrote *Introducing Microsoft .NET*. My daughters have learned to walk and talk. The twin towers have fallen. .NET has grown up. Maybe we all have. "We'll never laugh again," the columnist Mary McGrory told Daniel Patrick Moynihan after Kennedy's death. "We'll laugh again," Moynihan replied. "But we'll never be young again." I think I know now what he meant. Press deadline looms and I don't have time to philosophize further here. See the poetry section at the end Chapter 1 and my Contradiction in Chapter 6.

I do, however, need to take time to thank everyone who helped make this book possible. On the publishing side, Danielle Bird Voeller was my original acquisition editor and did great work in getting this book approved. Ben Ryan, with whom I worked on my first Microsoft Press book, *Understanding COM+*, is now a freelancer and picked up when Danielle went on maternity leave for her new daughter. Ben, great working with you again. Devon Musgrave started the editing process and quickly handed off to Karen Szall as the primary editor. Matt Carter helped slot the book into the Microsoft Press product line. Thanx to everyone.

Many people from the technical side helped review this book and correct its inaccuracies. It's especially difficult with a moving target as this piece of software currently is. For the .NET Framework in Chapter 2, I'll thank Jonathan Hawkins, Jamie Cool, Patrick Dussud, and Duncan MacKenzie. Erik Olsen and Brian Goldfarb gave invaluable advice on ASP.NET; Rebecca Dias and Keith Ballinger on Web services; Casey Chesnut on compact devices; Steve Lombardi, Chandhu Thota, and the whole MapPoint team on the MapPoint items. My thanks to all of them.

Finally, I need to thank my wife and daughters for putting up with Daddy closeting himself downstairs in his office when he should have been out playing with them.

Chapter 1
Introduction

> *I wanted the gold, and I sought it,*
> *I scrabbled and mucked like a slave.*
> *Was it famine or scurvy -- I fought it;*
> *I hurled my youth into a grave.*
> *I wanted the gold, and I got it --*
> *Came out with a fortune last fall, --*
> *Yet somehow life's not what I thought it,*
> *And somehow the gold isn't all.*
>
> -- Robert W. Service, "The Spell of the Yukon," stanza 0

The Wheels Keep Turning

The initial release of .NET caught people's interest.

The first release of Microsoft .NET revolutionized software development in the Microsoft world in a manner similar to the release of Windows 3.0. "Hey," people said, "this new piece of software actually does something useful." Early adopters rushed to market with the new apps that it let them write, and more cautious industries such as finance and insurance wrote prototypes and evaluation projects.

The next version has evolved based on user feedback.

Windows needed to evolve from 3.0 to 3.1—have its rougher edges sanded smooth—before it could become the world's favorite desktop platform. It needed user interface features such as OLE, developer aids such as common dialog boxes, and internal fixes such as a validation layer that reject bad parameters passed to the kernel before they could crash it. Most of all, it needed feedback from users and developers on what worked and what didn't, what they liked and what drove them into towering rages (Unrecoverable Application Error dialog box with an OK button only). While it started off as a far better product than Windows 3.0 ever dreamed of being, .NET still requires evolution based on user feedback before it can become the world's favorite development platform.

This book shows you the features that exist in the next release and gets you started with each of them.

This book describes the product code-named Whidbey, which is now known as Visual Studio 2005. It covers the underlying framework, ASP.NET, Web Services Enhancements and the Compact Framework. I don't go into the specifics of individual languages, such as the VB code snippet feature or C# iterators. I leave these to books on these specific languages. Nor do I, nor can I, delve into any topic too deeply. Each chapter, heck, each subsection within each chapter could support (and will probably get) a book of its own. The purpose of this book is to show you the features that exist and get you started with each one of them. If you think of nibbling off a corner of each chocolate candy in the boxed assortment so you can see which filling it contains and get an idea of its flavor, you'll have the right mental model. Perhaps I should call it the "Whitman's Sampler" of .NET books.[1]

Where We Are Now

Chapter 2 discusses version 2 of the .NET Framework.

The .NET Framework and its common language runtime continue to evolve. The new "generic" capability allows programmers to parameterize classes, that is, write code that handles in a type-safe manner objects of any class specified at compile time. The garbage collector has been modified to make it work better with unmanaged resources as well as managed ones. And ClickOnce deployment makes it much easier to install client programs. Chapter 2 discusses version 2 of the .NET Framework.

Chapter 3 discusses version 2 of ASP.NET.

The first version of ASP.NET brought website development capability within reach of the average application programmer, leastways mostly. The Web Forms architecture, and the high degree of prefabricated infrastructure on the back end, meant that developers could concentrate on their business logic instead of the site's underlying nuts and bolts. The second version continues this trend, providing even more prefabricated functionality for solving common infrastructural problems. For example, managing users (setting up accounts, retrieving lost passwords, and so on) is now completely prefabricated. There are many new Web Forms controls, extending that popular architecture, including codeless data access. Administration of the site, for example, assigning users to security roles, has been completely revamped to even my satisfaction. Master pages and themes allow you to enforce a common user interface look and feel across an entire site. Chapter 3 describes version 2 of ASP.NET.

Chapter 4 describes version 2 of the Web Services Enhancements.

The initial release of XML Web services provided basic connectivity. You shoved bytes into one end and the same bytes came out on the other end regardless of the platforms and operating systems used on either end. That's a powerful feature and an immense accomplishment, but it didn't solve the problems of user authentication, data integrity, or data privacy. We need to solve these before we can use XML Web services for any purpose involving personally identifiable data or macroscopic amounts of money. Because these problems apply equally to all business domains, we need them solved at an operating system level. And just to make it harder, we need our solution to work with non-Microsoft platforms, that being the entire point of XML Web services after all. The .NET Web Services Enhancements, version 2, provide these types of solutions. I discuss them in Chapter 4.

---

1 A Whitman's Sampler, for those who have never eaten one, is a box of assorted chocolates with a map on the lid that tells you which filling each one contains. You thus do not have to pick off a corner to avoid risking a mouthful of yucky coconut when you really wanted a lemon cream, or vice versa. This design works well until you eat enough of the chocolates that the remaining ones can slide out of the places to which the map assigns them. You therefore tend to consume the last half of the box in a single sitting.

Chapter 5 discusses the basic .NET Compact Framework, the Smartphone version of it, and the MapPoint Web Service.

Finally, .NET is gaining ground on platforms other personal computers, such as Pocket PCs and Smartphones. The former are useful in small (but potentially profitable) business niches—say, a traffic ticket entry system for walking police officers—because normal consumers don't want to carry a box of that size. The latter have much more mass market potential because every adult and teenager in the world already owns a cell phone and carries it everywhere. The .NET Compact Framework brings the benefits of rapid application development to these sub-PC platforms. The Pocket PC version has been around for a while, and I describe it for those who have never seen it. But the Smartphone version is new (I'm expecting my first prototype device that supports it just as this book goes to press) and exciting. The combination of smart mobile devices with global positioning opens up the possibility of location-based services, by which I mean services based on the user's current location, such as a map of the area where the user is standing. Microsoft's MapPoint Web Service provides access to the geographical data needed to make this sort of thing happen. Chapter 5 describes the basic .NET Compact Framework, the new Smartphone version of it, and the MapPoint Web Service.

This book contains chapters from other authors describing Yukon and Longhorn.

Visual Studio 2005 needs to be seen in the context of other evolutions of Windows that will ship at about the same time. To keep you up to date on them, my editor has cajoled, bribed, threatened, or otherwise wheedled two guest authors to contribute sample chapters from their own books to describe new parts of the platform, which you've known by the code names Yukon and Longhorn. You'll find these in appendixes at the back of this book.

Peter DeBetta contributes a chapter on the new SQL Server 2005 database system (Yukon).

Yukon is now called SQL Server 2005. It represents the next evolution of Microsoft's database product. The primary advance is that the database server will now host the .NET common language runtime, so you will be able to write stored procedures in any managed language, such as C# or VB. The barrier between database code and application code is getting more porous. Appendix A contains a chapter from the forthcoming book *Introducing Microsoft SQL Server 2005 for Developers* by Peter DeBetta (Microsoft Press, 2005).

Brent Rector contributes a chapter on the next version of the Windows operating system (Longhorn).

Longhorn is the code name for the next version of the Windows operating system, and it features tighter integration with all things .NET. The exact feature set hasn't been determined as this book goes to press, so I can't tell you what will be in it and what won't. Appendix B contains a chapter from the book *Introducing WinFX: The Application Programming Interface for the Next Generation of Microsoft Windows Code Name "Longhorn"* by Brent Rector (Microsoft Press, 2004). It deals with the new client-side file system.

About This Book

Sample programs and installation instructions are available on this book's website.

This book uses the basic style I've developed over my last four Microsoft Press books. I started with the format that David Chappell used so successfully in his book *Understanding ActiveX and OLE* (Microsoft Press, 1996): lots of explanations, lots of diagrams, and very little code in the text descriptions. As much as I liked David Chappell's book, I still felt hungry for code (as I often need a piece of chocolate cake to top off a meal of delicate sushi). I found myself writing code to help me understand his ideas, much as I wrote equations to understand the textual descriptions in Stephen Hawking's *A Brief History of Time*. (OK, I'm a geek.) So my book comes with working programs for all the examples I discuss. They're available on this book's website, which is *http://www.microsoftplatformahead.net*, naturally. Managers and architects will be able to read the book without drowning in code, while code-hungry programmers will still be able to slake their appetites. In a change from my previous works, most of the sample code I present in the text of this book is written in C#, because that's now what most of my readers are asking for. However, I've written all the samples in both C# and Visual Basic .NET, so devotees of either language can have what they want. Detailed system and installation requirements for the sample programs are available on the book's website.

Each chapter of this book presents a single topic from the top down.

Each chapter presents a single topic from the top down. I start by describing the architectural problem that needs to be solved. I then explain the high-level architecture of the infrastructure that .NET provides to help you solve that problem with a minimum amount of code. I next walk you through the simplest example I can imagine that employs the solution. Managers may want to stop reading after this section. I then continue with a discussion of finer points—other possibilities, boundary cases, and the like. Throughout, I've tried to follow Pournelle's Law, coined by Jerry Pournelle in his "Chaos Manor" computing column in the original *Byte* magazine, which states simply that, "You can never have too many examples."

Warning: Pre-Release Software

Any author of books on software needs to choose between timeliness and accuracy.

Modern software is the fastest changing field of human thought that ever has existed. Any book on it faces the dilemma of timeliness versus accuracy. If I write the book too early, the final product bears little resemblance to what the book describes. But if I wait until the product actually ships before I write it, then the product will be obsolete by the time the book actually hits the shelves.

I've based this book on the PDC Whidbey Alpha release so you can run the sample code.

I've written this book using PDC Whidbey Alpha version of the software because that's what most readers have today or can easily get. As of my press deadline (April Fool's Day 2004, a lovely piece of irony), Microsoft still has not announced when the official beta version will come out. I could get later builds of Visual Studio for the sample programs, which then would probably bear more resemblance to the finished product, but you couldn't build or run them. I've chosen to write code that you can actually play with. That means that some amount of this book will necessarily be out of date when the next version comes out. Where I've known that changes are likely, for example, classes moving to different namespaces, I've noted the likelihood of change in the text. I purposely haven't said what they're changing to, because that could also change. But at least you'll know which items you'll probably have to search for.

Another Song of Software

My readers liked Rudyard Kipling's poem in my last book.

My last book, *Introducing Microsoft .NET*, received many reviews, some of them good and some of them not. But no matter what anyone thought of my description of the software, they all loved my relating Rudyard Kipling's poem "McAndrew's Hymn" to the modern software industry. So when I stumbled across another poem that reminded me of this crazy geek business, I saved it for you.

I still don't like most modern poetry.

It still seems to me that many modern so-called poets just sprinkle random carriage returns through not-especially-good prose, with no apparent rhyme or rhythm, hoping thereby to magically transform it into poetry. Consider, for example, James Dickey (1923-1997), best known for his excellent novel *Deliverance*. His poetry is so widely respected that the University of South Carolina dedicated a memorial library to him. He served as the national Poet Laureate Consultant in Poetry to the Library of Congress from 1966 to 1968, an official government position. And yet, consider this excerpt from his poem "The Fiend":

> *He descends*
> *a medium-sized shadow*
> *while that one sleeps and*
> *turns*
> *In her high bed in loss*
> *as he goes limb by limb*
> *quietly down*
> *The trunk with one lighted side....*

Perhaps one of you readers can explain to me what makes this poetry instead of randomly indented prose. I'm sorry, but the emperor's clothes are not apparent to the miserable and uneducated wretch that I clearly must be.

But Robert W. Service is great, like Kipling.

Next to Kipling, I've always enjoyed the poetry of Robert W. Service (1874-1958). He's best known for poetry describing his beloved Yukon Territory, particularly during the Klondike gold rush of 1896-98. His poems have rhyme and rhythm, sometimes even better than Kipling. You've probably heard some of them before, maybe without knowing who wrote them. One of everyone's favorites, "The Cremation of Sam McGee," begins with these lines:

> *There are strange things done in the midnight sun*
> *By the men who moil for gold;*
> *The Arctic trails have their secret tales*
> *That would make your blood run cold;*
> *The Northern Lights have seen queer sights,*
> *But the queerest they ever did see*
> *Was that night on the marge of Lake Lebarge*
> *I cremated Sam McGee.*

I once used a poem of his as a literary amphetamine, and it worked.

My Outward Bound winter camping instructor used Service's poem "The Quitter" on our demoralized and flagging team one morning, after we'd just spent all our energy battering our way up the wrong damn mountain. I used it on my Harvard class last fall, when they were feeling the same way, bending (but not breaking, bless them) under the constant pounding of my homework assignments. Like a literary amphetamine, it fired them up long enough to get over the next hump. Here's an excerpt from it:

> *It's easy to cry that you're beaten – and die;*
> *It's easy to crawfish and crawl;*
> *But to fight and to fight when hope's out of sight –*
> *Why, that's the best game of them all!*
> *And though you come out of each gruelling bout,*
> *All broken and beaten and scarred,*
> *Just have one more try – it's dead easy to die,*
> *It's the keeping-on-living that's hard.*

The development process didn't motivate Kipling's McAndrew.

His poem "The Spell of the Yukon," first published in his 1907 book *Songs of a Sourdough*, sings to me of software, and not just because of the code name of SQL Server 2005. In "McAndrew's Hymn," Kipling celebrated the technology itself, and to some extent the operator of it. But McAndrew deliberately turned away from any hand in its development, saying:

> *Inventions? Ye must stay in port to mak' a patent pay.*
> *My Deeferential Valve-Gear taught me how that business lay,*
> *I blame no chaps wi' clearer head for aught they make or sell.*
> *I found that I could not invent an' look to these [his engines]–as well.*
> *So, wrestled wi' Apollyon–Nah!–fretted like a bairn–*
> *But burned the workin'-plans last run wi' all I hoped to earn.*
> *Ye know how hard an Idol dies, an' what that meant to me–*
> *E'en tak' it for a sacrifice acceptable to Thee. . . .*

But I think Service nailed it in "The Spell of the Yukon"

"The Spell of the Yukon" sings of the Klondike gold miners, the killer land in which they toiled, and how each changed the other. It rings true for me as an allegory for the software development process. After a titanic struggle, Service's character discovers that it's the process that moves him, not the product; the hunt and not the kill. That's you and me, my fellow geeks, as you'll see if you strip away the layers you've carefully constructed to hide your soul and look deeply enough inside. So I've opened each chapter with a stanza of this poem. If you read stanza 0 at the start of this chapter, then stanza 1 below, then the ones at the start of each chapter, you'll recite the entire poem in order. Here it is:

> *No! There's the land. (Have you seen it?)*
> *It's the cussedest land that I know,*
> *From the big, dizzy mountains that screen it*
> *To the deep, deathlike valleys below.*
> *Some say God was tired when He made it;*
> *Some say it's a fine land to shun;*
> *Maybe; but there's some as would trade it*
> *For no land on earth -- and I'm one.*

And if you're reading this book, you're probably another. Come on, let's go look at it.

Chapter 2
.NET Framework Version 2.0

You come to get rich (damned good reason);
  You feel like an exile at first;
You hate it like hell for a season,
  And then you are worse than the worst.
It grips you like some kinds of sinning;
  It twists you from foe to a friend;
It seems it's been since the beginning;
  It seems it will be to the end.

— *Robert W. Service, "The Spell of the Yukon," stanza 2*

Problem Background

Developers loved the high level of abstraction and pre-fabrication of the .NET Framework, but version 1 of anything is incomplete.

The .NET Framework was fantastically successful at its task of providing a robust yet easy-to-use object services platform. The fundamental architectural principle on which it rests, commonality of implementation among all components and applications, has been vindicated. Prefabricated infrastructure, such as garbage collection, accomplished the elusive combination of faster development with fewer bugs. The Framework provided a sound foundation for the higher level functionality built on top of it, such as ASP.NET and Web Services. But version 1 of anything is necessarily incomplete. What did version 1 not have in it?

Arrays can hold objects of any class, but we usually want any particular array to hold objects of only one class.

The largest omission in the Framework's object services is the inability to parameterize object types, similar to the template mechanism of C++ or Java. That might not mean much at first glance, especially to non-programmers, but here's what I mean and why it's important. Suppose I have an array, an object of class System.Array. That array is defined as holding objects of the universal base class System.Object, which means that it can hold any .NET object in existence. This is handy because we don't have to develop a special array to hold each class of object that we have to deal with. But it's rare that we use any particular array to hold objects of more than one class. Even though any element can hold an object of any class, we usually want all elements of an array to hold objects of the same class—strings, fish, birds, whatever. This means that storing an object of a different class, say a fish into an array of birds, probably represents an error in our program logic, even though the array class allows it. We'd like a way for the compiler to catch such errors.

We'd like to be able to pass classes as parameters for better type fidelity.

The only way we can currently do this is by writing our own wrappers for every method on the existing array class. This effort would entail a large amount of repetitive infrastructural development work. And if there's one thing you should have learned from everything I've ever written about .NET, it's that large amounts of repetitive infrastructural work belong in the operating system, not your program logic. We would like a mechanism that would allow us, when we create an array, to pass it the type of object that we want it to hold and have it reject attempts to make it hold anything else. We would like to somehow tell it, "Hey, I know you can hold anything, but in this case, I want you to restrict yourself to holding only birds." Since the compiler would know the class that the array holds, we like to assign an object we fetch from it directly into a variable of the correct type without needing to cast it. The compiler would also know if the array was holding a value type (an object initially allocated on the stack and passed by value, such as ints, structs, and so on), so we could allocate the correct amount of storage to hold it by value in the array. This would allow us to avoid boxing of value types (automatically allocating space on the managed heap to convert them into reference types), which consumes time and heap space and increases the frequency of garbage collections. Developers of this super-smart array class would like to write the code only once and have it magically work with any class that the client tells it to. And we'd like to easily use this mechanism in writing any class, not just an array, that needs to hold another potentially varying class. (Spoiler: Even though it sounds complicated, we actually do get all of this fairly easily, as I'll show you.)

Garbage collection is a wonderful thing for pure managed objects.

Automatic memory management through garbage collection is probably the most universally loved feature of the .NET Framework. The common language runtime (CLR) determines when it's running low on managed heap memory and triggers a garbage collection that identifies unused objects and reclaims their memory. This technique prevents both memory leaks and premature object destruction, removing a major infrastructural headache and money sink from application developers. It works wonderfully for pure managed objects, by which I mean objects that do not wrap any sort of unmanaged (non-.NET) resource.

However, most of the programs being written today contain at least some managed objects that wrap unmanaged resources.

Unfortunately, in real-life development today, our programs almost never contain only pure managed objects. When I spoke at Tech Ed Barcelona in the summer of 2003, I asked my attendees to raise their hands if they were writing pure .NET applications, with no legacy COM objects or other unmanaged code, and got only 5 or 6 hands out of 700 people in the audience. It's much more common that we use at least some objects that are managed wrappers for unmanaged resources, perhaps a large amount of unmanaged memory, or a small but scarce resource such as a database connection. Even some objects that you think of as purely managed, such as System.Drawing.Bitmap, are implemented internally as a small managed wrapper over a much larger unmanaged memory block containing the image.

The CLR doesn't know how to identify a shortage of unmanaged resources.

A properly written wrapper object contains a finalizer, a method which frees the unmanaged resource when the garbage collector sweeps up the managed wrapper, thereby avoiding a permanent leakage. The problem is that the unmanaged resource isn't released until the next garbage collection, and the CLR can't recognize a shortage of the unmanaged resources in order to trigger that collection. It responds only to the managed heap and doesn't know what else to look at. The managed heap might have plenty of space remaining to allocate the wrappers, but you might be fresh out of the database connections that they would wrap. A garbage collection would reclaim them, but until it happens, you're stuck, as shown in Figure 2-1.

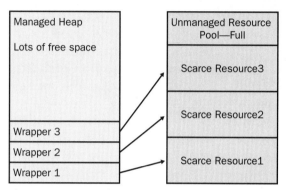

Figure 2-1   Lots of managed heap space but out of an unmanaged resource pool.

We'd like it to recognize shortages of unmanaged resources as well as managed heap memory.

To clean up these unmanaged resources, class designers implement the IDisposable interface. Calling its Dispose method tells an object, "OK, I'm done. Go ahead and release your unmanaged resources." Like seat belts or birth control, this design approach only works reliably if you remember to use it every time. Clients forget to call it, and we're back to the old days of memory leaks and unwanted pregnancies. We'd like a way to tell the garbage collector how to respond to the scarcity of our unmanaged resources as it now does for managed resources, so that it can run to free the unreachable managed wrappers that in turn free the unmanaged resources.

Installing client applications on a user's PC is difficult and expensive.

One of the major costs of software ownership is deploying applications to users' machines. A rich client application, running on the customer's PC, can not only have a much better user interface than a browser-based application, but can also run when the user isn't connected to the Internet. But getting the program onto the client's machine and properly installed is much more difficult than it sounds, causing developers to accept the second-class browser user interface in preference to dealing with the hassles of installing a good one. We'd like a prefabricated way to make installing rich client applications easier.

We need an easy and safe way of installing them.

Having a trained administrator physically go to and touch a user's PC is prohibitively expensive, so our new mechanism needs to work properly with untrained users.

Because these users don't know what's safe and what isn't, we need to make sure that our installation mechanism can't open any security holes, and we need it to run with the security restrictions that most ordinary non-administrator users have. We need a way to specify the prerequisites of our new program, for example, the version of the .NET Framework it requires, and install them if they're not present. We need our new installation not to break any existing applications and ideally not be broken by installation of future applications. We'd like it to look and feel like a desktop application, with a Start menu entry and an entry in the Add/Remove Programs list on Control Panel.

We'd also like easy and safe handling of program updates.

Checking for and installing updates to existing programs poses a similar problem. We'd like our programs to be able to automatically check for updates and notify the user. We'd like it to be easy to install the updates when the user chooses to. We'd like a way to specify when an update is required and have the application refuse to run without it, say, to enforce the installation of the latest security update. Remember how lots of users (including me, I'm ashamed to say) didn't install the service pack that fixed SQL Server's Slammer worm until they got hit by it, and the mess that resulted? Earlier installation of fixes can choke off an epidemic. Finally, not every upgrade is a good one. Despite the best efforts of developers, a new update sometimes breaks an existing behavior that we care about. Sometimes user interface designers get it wrong, usually because the designers forget that they're not building user interfaces for themselves, and users hate the results. (One word: Clippy.[1]) We'd like to be able to roll back to the previous version of an application if the user wants to (provided, of course, that the update isn't required).

We'd like a few other miscellaneous features.

As long as we're compiling a wish list for the next version, we might as well put everything we want on it. Most developers will consider these requests minor, but there are always a few to whom this or that particular feature is life or death for what their application needs to do. ("You may be only one feature in a whole operating system, but you may be the whole operating system to one poor geek." Or something like that.) We'd like a better native image compiler, so that we can generate object code from the MSIL just once on installation time and not re-JIT our programs every time we run them. The existing one produces code that is often slower than JIT code. We'd like the console API improved to the point we could write space invaders for it. We'd like to be able to use the serial port from the .NET Framework, which is not built in and has hitherto required expensive workarounds. And we'd like easily managed FTP file transfer as well.

---

1 I am not alone in detesting that vile, Gollum-like creature. As lawyers Dahlia Lithwick and Brandt Goldstein wrote in *Me v. Everybody: Absurd Contracts for an Absurd World* (Workman Publishing, 2003, ISBN 0-7611-2389-X): "3. The Maniacal-Paper-Clip-With-Eyebrows Provision. You will delete/disable/destroy whatever it is that allows that inane little bastard to leap around the bottom right-hand corner of my screen, emitting what can only be described as a mechanical fart and incessantly observing: 'I see that you're writing a ransom note ...' or assuming that I wish it to turn all my letters into spreadsheets and my correspondence into numbered lists."

Solution Architecture

Version 2.0 of the .NET Framework is an evolutionary improvement.

Version 2.0 of the .NET Framework represents an evolutionary improvement over previous versions. It doesn't have the major dislocations and learning curves that programmers encountered in moving from COM-based programming to .NET. It reminds me very much of the transition from Windows 3.0 to 3.1 so many, many bottles of beer ago. I remember user interface standardization features such as a common dialog box that any application could use for getting the user's selection of a file to open, features for easier programming such as a function-based wrapper for dynamic data exchange, and many bug fixes under the hood where I didn't see them but where my code crashed less than it used to. It's the release that takes the original good idea that people have been using for a while and smooths it off for the rest of the world.

Many of the changes are at such a low level that this book can't cover them.

The Framework has evolved in similar ways. Its basic structure is still the same as it was on its first release in 2002. For example, the notion of class inheritance regardless of source code language hasn't changed, nor has the universal base class System.Object. Many changes that have been made are at so low a level that few application programmers will ever see them. For example, the algorithm for garbage collection has undergone some internal revisions so that it better detects a program's change from startup mode to steady-state run mode and tunes its collection thresholds appropriately. You won't see this sort of change, but it should make your program run a little better. Usually, anyway. The remaining changes are generally new ways to make programming smoother.

The Framework supports generics, which allow classes to be parameterized.

Version 2.0 of the .NET Framework supports parameterizing classes by a mechanism called "generics." This looks and feels very much like the template mechanism in C++ or Java. The designer of a class, such as System.Collections.Generic.List, can accept a type as a parameter by using a special syntax, as shown in Listing 2-1. The client programmer is passing the String type, saying, "Here, create me a list that holds only strings, please." Any attempt to store an object other than a string in that list will cause a compiler error. The Framework's generic mechanism makes it very easy for the generic class designer to work with any type that the client passes. It eliminates boxing of value types and casting. It works properly across all languages and makes IntelliSense prompts more specific and therefore more useful. The Framework both provides a set of collection classes that use this mechanism and exposes the mechanism itself for use in writing your own classes. The first example of this chapter demonstrates the generic mechanism.

Listing 2-1   Passing a type parameter to a generic class.

```
// Create a new generic List, telling it to accept only objects
// of class String

System.Collections.Generic.List <String> StringList =
    new System.Collections.Generic.List<String> ();
```

The garbage collector now contains methods to increase the frequency of collections to recover unmanaged resources inside managed wrappers.

Version 2.0 contains several techniques that allow the garbage collector to better recover unmanaged resources. The garbage collector itself contains two new methods: AddMemoryPressure and ReleaseMemoryPressure. The former tells the garbage collector to increase the frequency of its collections because there are likely to be a lot of wrappers of expensive unmanaged resources around waiting to be reclaimed, and the latter undoes this action. A small managed object that wraps a large amount of unmanaged memory will call the former just before it allocates the unmanaged memory and the latter just after it releases it. It basically tells the collector to treat the small managed object as being larger than its actual size would warrant, thus reflecting the unmanaged resources that it wraps. You pass these methods an integer parameter telling it how much to increase or decrease the pressure. I demonstrate the memory pressure methods in the second example in this chapter.

The behavior for quantized resources is different.

The second resource recovery mechanism takes a different, more deterministic approach. Often the size of the unmanaged resource isn't continuously variable as it is with bitmaps of different sizes. Instead, it's quantized, by which I mean it occurs in discrete chunks of roughly equal cost, of which you only have a certain non-expandable number. The classic example of this is database connections. You can create them or fetch them from a pool, up to some non-negotiable limit. If the client properly calls Dispose on the managed wrapper, the unmanaged object gets released and is available to the next caller. But if the client forgets, an all-too-common occurrence, the managed wrapper sits around holding the scarce unmanaged resource until the next garbage collection, and you can run out of the unmanaged resource before that happens. The solution to this is to track the supply of the unmanaged resource and force a garbage collection when it runs low, thus, hopefully, recovering the unmanaged resources held by managed objects that have become garbage.

The HandleCollector class tracks the supply of expensive handles and forces a garbage collection when it exceeds a specified threshold.

Version 2.0 now contains a class called System.Runtime.InteropServices.HandleCollector. This is an administrative object that tracks the supply of an unmanaged resource and triggers a garbage collection when it runs low. When you create an instance of it, you tell it the maximum number of unmanaged objects ("handles") that are available in your application. Your managed wrapper class then informs the HandleCollector every time it allocates a handle (generally in its constructor) and every time it releases one (generally in its finalizer). If the HandleCollector's count of outstanding handles reaches the limit that you've set for it, it triggers a garbage collection to recover the wrappers and thus the handles that they wrap. If you never forget to call a wrapper's Dispose method, the HandleCollector will never hit its limit and you'll never see an unnecessary garbage collection. On the other hand, if you'd rather forget all about Dispose for the objects you're tracking and let the HandleCollector take care of them, so be it. As you'll see in this chapter's third example, it tunes its algorithm to match the number of handles recovered with each collection.

ClickOnce deployment allows users to easily and safely install programs on their machines.

The Framework now supports a feature called ClickOnce deployment. (The user occasionally has to click twice, as we'll see, but that's still what they call it.) This is a mechanism that allows a developer or an administrator to publish an application to an Internet or network share for easy deployment to a user's machine. Users can see a Web page that allows them to click and install the prerequisites or the application itself. ClickOnce downloads and installs the programs on the user's machine in a safe way, not allowing any sort of changes that would cause any other program to break. It doesn't allow an application to modify any files other than its own directory or install anything into the GAC. Visual Studio provides a default implementation of ClickOnce, but it's actually managed by an underlying set of objects in the System.Deployment namespace, so it's very easy to customize its behavior if you'd like.

ClickOnce supports automatic upgrades to applications as well.

ClickOnce allows an application publisher to set an application's update policy, specifying how often the program should check for updates to itself. The publisher can then place updates on that share, using the standard Framework versioning mechanism to specify the version of each update. When the program checks for updates and finds one, it prompts the user to decide whether to install it. The administrator can also mark an update as required, in which case the application will not run until the update is installed. ClickOnce saves the previous version when installing an update; if the user doesn't like a non-required update, he can roll back to the previous version by using Control Panel. The fourth example shows ClickOnce deployment.

A few more miscellaneous features have been added.

Version 2.0 contains a number of other updates, which time and space don't permit me to deal with in this book. The Framework has a new native image generator, which produces better code than the previous one did. You'll still need to check both JIT and NGEN code to see which is faster. Console IO has been upgraded significantly. And Framework now contains managed classes that deal with the serial port and FTP.

Simplest Example: Generics

A generic example starts here.

To demonstrate the generic features of the version 2 framework, I wrote the simplest example I could think of. You can download the code from this book's website, *http://www.microsoftplatformahead.com*, and work along with me. This book shows only C# in its printed listings, but the online sample code shows both VB and C#. I used the Whidbey alpha PDC edition of Visual Studio because I thought that's what most people had or could get. I created a standard Windows Forms project to hold my code. The user interface doesn't really do anything, so I won't bother to show it here.

An ArrayList holds objects of any class.

Listing 2-2 shows the situation without generics. Suppose I'm writing a drawing program and I need an array of objects of class Point. I create a standard ArrayList (an expandable array, as opposed to System.Array which is fixed length). ArrayList holds any object that derives from the universal base class System.Object, which means anything at all. I create an object of class Point and store it in the ArrayList, which is correct program behavior. I then create an object of class Color and add it to the ArrayList. This isn't correct behavior; instead, it's a result of a logic error. But the ArrayList allows it because both Point and Color classes derive from System.Object. A collection occasionally does need to hold objects of unrelated classes, for example, a property bag. But it's much more common to want an array of only one class, such as Point. We'd like to somehow catch the logic error we made in storing a Color where a Point should be.

Listing 2-2   ArrayList without generics holds objects of any class.

```
private void button1_Click(object sender, System.EventArgs e)
{        // Create a standard ArrayList

        ArrayList al = new ArrayList ( ) ;

        // Create a point, store it in the ArrayList.
        // Boxing takes place automatically

        Point p = new Point (5, 10) ;
        al.Add (p) ;

        // Create a color, store it in the ArrayList

        Color c = Color.AliceBlue;
        al.Add(c);

        // Fetch the Point from the ArrayList.
        // Casting is required.

        Point q = (Point) al[0];

}
```

The term "generic" can be confusing in this context.

To fix this problem, we can use a somewhat misnamed "generic collection." I say it's misnamed because we define it to hold a specific class. It seems to me that the original ArrayList should be called a generic collection because it holds anything at all and you can't change its behavior. We're now taking a so-called generic class and defining it to hold only Points. I think it should be called something like "restricted collection" or "specific collection." Perhaps to differentiate it from collections hard-written to hold only objects of certain classes, I might call it a "parameterized specific collection" or a "compile-specified collection." But then, they didn't ask me what to name it.

The generic List class accepts a type as a parameter and then holds objects of only that type.

Version 2.0 of the .NET Framework contains a mechanism for passing a class to the compiler as a parameter. It also contains a number of collection classes that use this technique to make collections whose contents I can specify when I create them. Consider the code shown in Listing 2-3. Instead of an ArrayList, I create an object of class System.Collections.Generic.List, passing it in its angle brackets the class that I want it to hold, in this case Point. (Despite the difference in name, the List is the generic version of the ArrayList.) The compiler then knows that this particular List should hold only Point objects. Attempting to assign a Color into it causes a compiler error. That's why that line is commented out in the listing. Try uncommenting and compiling it if you don't believe me.

Listing 2-3   List using generics is restricted to hold Point objects.

```
private void button2_Click(object sender, System.EventArgs e)
{
    // Create a new generic List, telling it to accept only objects
    // of class Point

    System.Collections.Generic.List <Point> l =
            new System.Collections.Generic.List<Point> ();

    // Create a new Point, add it to the list. This works.
    // Boxing does NOT occur

    Point p = new Point(6, 7);
    l.Add(p);

    // Create a new color

    Color c = Color.AntiqueWhite;

    // Attempting to add the color to the list that accepts only
    // Points causes a compiler error. This line does NOT work.

//    l.Add(c);

    // Fetch the Point from the ArrayList. No cast needed.

    Point q = l[0];

}
```

Using generics avoids boxing and casting.

Using the generic List instead of the System.Object-holding ArrayList gives me other advantages as well. The Point object is a value type, which means that it is initially allocated on the stack. Assigning it into the ArrayList requires converting it into a reference object on the managed heap, an operation known as *boxing* (in the sense of containerization, not pugilism). Fetching it out again at the end of the method requires the opposite operation, known as *unboxing*. You can see these instructions in the MSIL shown in Figure 2-2. These operations happen automatically without my having to write any code, but they do take time and cause more garbage collections. In the generic example, the boxing and unboxing operations are absent. I'll explain why we don't need them in the next paragraph. Finally, you'll note that the generic example doesn't need a cast when I fetch the object from the List because the compiler already knows what type it is. The cast doesn't require any MSIL instructions, but putting it in the wrong place is another source of logic errors in the source code, which we will not be sorry to lose.

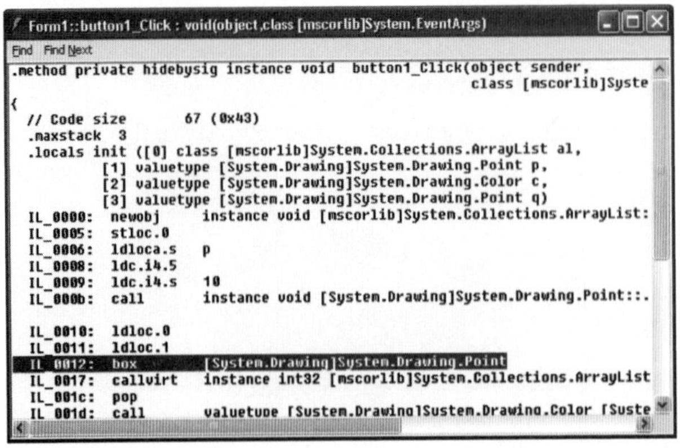

Figure 2-2   MSIL showing boxing instruction for non-generic ArrayList.

The designer of a generic class provides type parameters that the user of the class passes.

You can use the generic technique for writing your own classes as well. I've written a class called GenericHolder, shown in Listing 2-4. I use angle brackets to designate the *type parameter*, which is where the client passes the type at compile time. (You can have as many type parameters as you want, but beware of confusion if you use more than one or two.) I've named my type parameter "TypeTheClientToldMeToHold" in this example so that you understand what I'm doing with it. I use that parameter where I would normally use a hard-wired type, such as int or double. You can see that in the constructor I use the type parameter and pop up a message box showing what it is. You can see that I declare a variable to hold an instance of it, and accessor methods for setting it and fetching it. The compiler magically takes the type the user passes in constructing the class and uses whatever it is. I think this is the reason for the name "generic." You write your code for handling objects without regard to the types involved. The designers of the mechanism named it based on their internal implementation, and not that of the user.

Listing 2-4   Writing our own generic class.

```
public class GenericHolder < TypeTheClientToldMeToHold >
{
        // At construction time, show a dialog box telling the
        // user the type we currently hold

        public GenericHolder()
        {
                MessageBox.Show("Type I hold is: "
                    + typeof (TypeTheClientToldMeToHold).ToString());
        }

        // This member variable magically holds whatever type
        // the client tells us to hold.
```

```
        private TypeTheClientToldMeToHold objectThatIHold;

        public void Add (TypeTheClientToldMeToHold obj)
        {
            objectThatIHold = obj ;
        }

        public TypeTheClientToldMeToHold Fetch()
        {
        return objectThatIHold ;
        }
    }
```

More Complex Example: Memory Pressure

A memory pressure example program starts here.

I've written a sample application to demonstrate the AddMemoryPressure and RemoveMemoryPressure methods of the garbage collector. The client is shown in Figure 2-3. When you click the button, the client program creates an object and immediately lets it go out of scope and become garbage, as shown in Listing 2-5. The objects log their creation and finalization to the list box so you can see when they come and go.

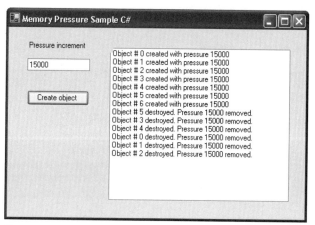

Figure 2-3   Memory pressure sample client program.

Listing 2-5   Memory pressure sample client code.

```
    private void button1_Click(object sender, System.EventArgs e)
    {
        // Create an object with the specified resource pressure

        SmallWrapperOfBigUnmanaged foo = new
            SmallWrapperOfBigUnmanaged(Convert.ToInt32(textBox1.Text));
    }
```

You call AddMemoryPressure to increase garbage collection frequency and RemoveMemoryPressure to decrease it.

The objects call AddMemoryPressure in their constructors, passing the integer entered by the user. They call RemoveMemoryPressure in their finalizers, passing the same integer. Listing 2-6 shows these calls. It's important to balance the added and removed pressures so that the collector properly understands its current state. I think you need to wrap these calls up in a class, as I've done here, so application programmers can't forget to call them or mess up the balancing.

Listing 2-6 Object calling AddMemoryPressure and RemoveMemoryPressure.

```
private int MyPressure ;

public SmallWrapperOfBigUnmanaged (int pressure)
{
        // Remember the pressure we're given

        MyPressure = pressure;

        // Add that amount of pressure

        if (MyPressure != 0)
        {
                System.GC.AddMemoryPressure(MyPressure);
        }

        // Inform the user (code omitted)
}

~SmallWrapperOfBigUnmanaged()
{
        //Remove the amount of pressure we added earlier

        if (MyPressure != 0)
        {
                System.GC.RemoveMemoryPressure(MyPressure);
        }

        // Inform the user (code omitted)

}
```

The meaning of the pressure parameter is not very clear.

The documentation doesn't state exactly what the integer parameter means. Many of the samples pass the size in bytes of the unmanaged resource wrapped by managed object. However, the one coherent sentence I can find in the documentation states: "The value of pressure need not be merely a measure of the unmanaged memory used by a resource; the value you specify reflects the importance of the resource and the degree to which it is constrained, not just its size." It seems to be a general-purpose garbage collector frequency increaser.

What effect, then, does memory pressure have on garbage collection frequency? I set out to measure it with the sample program. It logs object creation and finalization, so you can see when the garbage collections take place. I set the parameter to various values and recorded the average number of object creations required to trigger a garbage collection. Table 2-1 summarizes the results.

Table 2-1   Measuring Memory Pressure

Memory Pressure parameter, per object	Number of object allocations required to trigger a garbage collection, average of first 10 collections
(not called – normal behavior)	7.2
1	8.5
1K	8.5
10K	8.0
15K	3.9
20K	3.0
50K	2.0
100K	2.0
1000K	2.0

The range of effective parameters seems to be quite narrow.

I found no significant effect of passing 10K or less per object. The garbage collection frequency was about the same as it was without any pressure-related calls. Between 10,000 and 20,000, the frequency of garbage collection increased by a factor of three. Over 20,000, it didn't increase by much because it was already collecting on almost every other object allocation. Your mileage, of course, may vary widely. The behavior of the garbage collector in the Windows Forms case may be very different from that in, say, an ASP.NET server application. And it wouldn't surprise me at all to see the behavior change from this early alpha version to the final release. You need to check your specific application to see what behavior you get.

This seems a little vague for production use.

I'm not sure how useful this feature will actually be in production because you're never sure exactly how much any particular call affects the garbage collection frequency. It is probably handiest when the size of the unmanaged resource can vary greatly within the same managed wrapper class, such as a bitmap that can be tiny or enormous. Using these methods allows you to say, "Collect more frequently because this one's much bigger than the others." If your unmanaged objects are all of roughly the same size or cost, then I think you'll prefer more determinism. We can get that from the HandleCollector class, which I'll discuss next.

More Complex Example: Handle Collector

A HandleCollector sample program starts here.

The main drawback to the Dispose design pattern used for freeing unmanaged resources is the fact that the client can forget to call it, and frequently does, especially since garbage collection makes the rest of memory management so easy. Providing a mechanism that can save bad programmers from leaking away unmanaged resources (albeit temporarily, until the next garbage collection) while not penalizing good programmers is always tricky. But the HandleCollector class actually accomplishes this. It was originally designed as an internal framework class to track the usage of GDI objects in Windows Forms. These could be in very short supply, as few as 5 HDC objects machine wide in Windows 95. Now it's been made available as a general utility class for all Framework applications. I've written a sample program to demonstrate the handle collector class. The client program is shown in Figure 2-4.

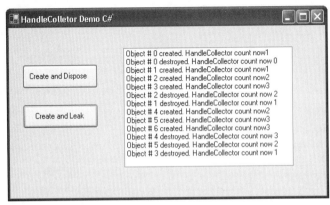

Figure 2-4   Handle Collector sample program.

My class contains a static HandleCollector object to maintain the count of this class and force garbage collections to recover unmanaged resources when necessary.

Listing 2-7 shows the code for a class that I call WrapperOfExpensiveHandles. In it, I declare and construct a static (shared) member variable of class HandleCollector to track the objects of this class. You can have as many instances of the HandleCollector as you care to, each tracking the status of a different class of object. In addition to the name of the HandleCollector object, I pass it the initial threshold, which is the minimum count at which to force a garbage collection, and the maximum threshold, which is the maximum value the count can reach before forcing a garbage collection. As you'll see, the HandleCollector will tune its operation between these two values. For the purpose of this demonstration, I set the minimum threshold to 2 and the maximum to 5.

Listing 2-7   Class using HandleCollector.

```csharp
public class WrapperOfExpensiveHandles : IDisposable
{

    // Create a handle collector

    private static HandleCollector hc = new HandleCollector (
        "WrapperOfExpensiveHandles",  // collection name
            2,              // initial threshold
            5) ;            // maximum threshold

    public WrapperOfExpensiveHandles ()
    {
```

```
        // Signal the handle collector that a new handle
        // is about to be fetched

        hc.Add();

        // Pretend that we now fetch a handle to
        // an expensive unmanaged resource

        // Inform the user (code omitted)
    }

    // This method gets called from both the finalizer and Dispose

    private void MyOwnCleanup ( )
    {
        // Signal the handle collector that we're about to free an
        // expensive, unmanaged resource.

        hc.Remove();

        // Pretend that we now release the handle to
        // an expensive, unmanaged resource

        // Inform the user (code omitted)

    }
}
```

I increment the HandleCollectors count when I acquire the expensive resource and decrement it when I release it.

In the WrapperOfExpensiveHandles constructor, you can see that I call the Handle-Collector's Add method, incrementing its internal count. This is where I would acquire the expensive resource in a production application, as the comment explains. I also log the construction to the client's list box so you can see it. The HandleCollec-tor's Count property allows me to read its internal count. The object's finalizer and Dispose method both call the method MyOwnInternalCleanup, a convenient location for cleanup code regardless of whether the cleanup is caused by the garbage collec-tor's finalizer or the client properly calling Dispose. In it, I call the HandleCollector's Remove method, decrementing its internal count, and also log it to the client's list box for you to see. This is where I would release the expensive resource in a production application. The class designer has to properly match calls to Add with calls to Release to properly track the usage of the scarce handles.

Correctly following the IDisposable design pattern doesn't force any unneeded garbage collections.

The client code is shown in Listing 2-8. Clicking the Create And Dispose button invokes the top function. This creates an object of my wrapper class and properly calls Dispose on it, as a good programmer should. Clicking this button once produced the first two lines in the list box in Figure 2-4. You can see that an object got created, at which time the HandleCollector's count was 1, and then got destroyed, at which time it dropped back to zero.

Listing 2-8 Client code for HandleCollector sample.

```
private void button1_Click(object sender, System.EventArgs e)
{
        // Create a new object of the wrapper class. This increments the
        // HandleCollector's count.

        WrapperOfExpensiveHandles woeh =
                new WrapperOfExpensiveHandles ();

        // Pretend to do something useful with object.
        // Correctly dispose of object. This frees internal unmanaged
        // resources and decrements the HandleCollector's count.

        woeh.Dispose();
}

private void button2_Click(object sender, System.EventArgs e)
{
        // Create a new object of the wrapper class. This increments the
        // HandleCollector's count.

        WrapperOfExpensiveHandles woeh =
                new WrapperOfExpensiveHandles();

        // Pretend to do something useful with object.

        // Incorrectly fail to call Dispose. Internal unmanaged resources
        // are not freed. HandleCollector's count not decremented.

}
```

The HandleCollector forces a garbage collection when its threshold is exceeded.

The bottom function simulates the rude behavior of a bad programmer. It creates an object of the wrapper class but forgets to free it. The object becomes garbage, but the garbage collector doesn't know that it contains an expensive handle. The next five lines in Figure 2-4 are caused by clicking this button three times. The first two clicks each create an object and increment the HandleCollector's count. When I click the button a third time, creating the new object bumps the HandleCollector's count up to 3, over the initial collection threshold. The HandleCollector forces a garbage collection, which calls the finalizers on the first two objects, invoking our cleanup code in which we would free the scarce handles. You will note, if you continue to run the program, that the HandleCollector tunes the intervals between garbage collections by allowing the count to reach 4 and even 5 before forcing one.

The HandleCollector doesn't remove the need for programmer thought and discipline.

Despite optimizations, the overhead of a garbage collection can be high because the garbage collector has to examine the entire managed heap. I find the HandleCollector design especially elegant because it doesn't force unnecessary garbage collections if the client programmer follows the rules and properly calls Dispose at the right time. It doesn't penalize good drivers for the actions of bad drivers. I need to point out, however, that using a HandleCollector doesn't increase the total number of handles available or force you to let go of one that you're actually still using. It only recovers the ones that you've finished with but forgot to Dispose. If your program really needs six handles in use at one time and the scarce resource only allows five, the HandleCollector isn't going to help you.

More Complex Example: ClickOnce Deployment

A ClickOnce deployment sample starts here.

I wrote a sample program that demonstrates the use of ClickOnce deployment. It was surprisingly easy to make it work in the default manner and even customize it. The client application is shown in Figure 2-5. It displays the version number that it reads from its own metadata so you know which version you have. While I demonstrate the feature of automatically checking for updates, I also show you how to use the ClickOnce object model to customize its behavior. That's why it has the Check For Updates button in the middle.

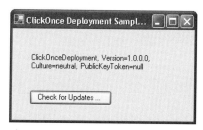

Figure 2-5   ClickOnce Deployment sample program.

You set the deployment project properties with a dialog box.

I wrote the simple Windows Forms application, setting the version number in the AssemblyInfo.cs file to 1.0.0.0. I next needed to set the properties that govern publishing the deployment project. I do this by selecting Project – Properties from the main menu and selecting Configuration Properties – Publish from the tree view, as shown in Figure 2-6. It lets me specify the location to which to publish and whether it should be installed as a stand-alone application on the client or run directly from the Web. (I chose the former.) You can specify the prerequisites that the program must have (Figure 2-7) and whether to prompt the user for them. (Don't. The user shouldn't have to think. There's even a book on user interface design entitled *Don't Make Me Think: A Common Sense Approach to Web Usability*, by Steve Krug.)

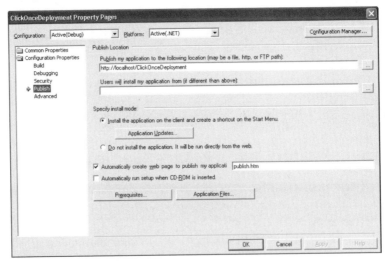

Figure 2-6   Publishing properties dialog box.

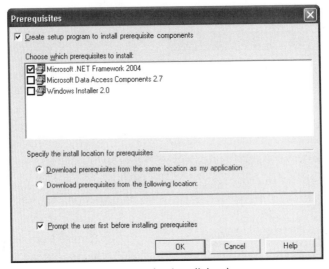

Figure 2-7   Prerequisites selection dialog box.

Visual Studio copies the deployment package onto a network share and provides a Web page for the user to view and click.

To actually place the deployment package onto a network share, I then right-clicked the project and selected Publish. This leads to a wizard allowing me to override some of the properties that I previously specified. It then copies the needed files up to the designated network location, as shown in Figure 2-8. The file Publish.htm, shown in the browser in Figure 2-9, is what the users actually see. It's pretty rudimentary, but you can easily spiff it up with any HTML editor. Clicking the Prerequisites link runs the Setup.exe program, which installs version 2 of the .NET Framework, if necessary. Otherwise, the client-side deployment code won't be on the target machine and the rest of the process I'm about to describe won't work. This is why I said earlier that sometimes you need to click twice. But that should only happen once.

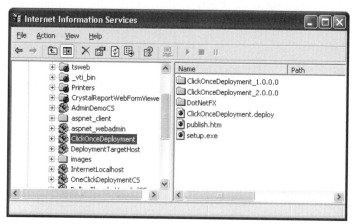

Figure 2-8   ClickOnce deployment network share containing two versions.

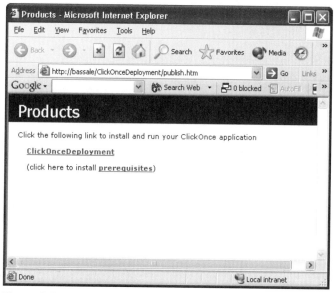

Figure 2-9   User Web page for ClickOnce deployment.

Publishing the project creates the manifest file and puts it and the others on a share.

Clicking the application name downloads and runs the .deploy file. This is an XML document, written in a specific problem domain vocabulary, that tells the client-side framework which version and which codebase to install. Each version of the application has its own folder on the network share. Each contains an application manifest that specifies the needed files and security settings for that particular version. The manifest files are somewhat opaque, so I won't bother showing listings of them here, but you can examine them in this book's downloadable code samples.

The user installs the software on his client machine by clicking the link.

When the user clicks on the deployment link, the client-side Framework code executes the instructions in the manifest files. The user will see a confirmation dialog box, as shown in Figure 2-10, then a progress bar showing the ongoing state of the deployment. (It will be quick in this sample program.) When the deployment is finished, she'll see a Startup menu item as for any other desktop program.

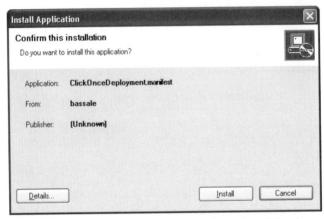

Figure 2-10   ClickOnce installation confirmation dialog box.

You specify the update behavior in the properties dialog box.

ClickOnce also handles updates. The publisher specifies the program's update-checking behavior using the dialog box shown in Figure 2-11. This information gets placed in the deployment manifest. You can specify whether the program checks for updates, and if so, how often, and at startup time or in the background. You can also mark an update as required, which means that the program won't run unless the update is installed. You should use this only for updates which are dangerous if not applied, such as a security hole fix. If someone made Clippy a required update, I think the designer would have to change his name, have plastic surgery, and flee to Paraguay. When the program runs, it checks for updates. If found, it offers you the choice, as shown in Figure 2-12. It then downloads and installs them. The user can roll back an unwanted update using Control Panel, as shown in Figure 2-13.

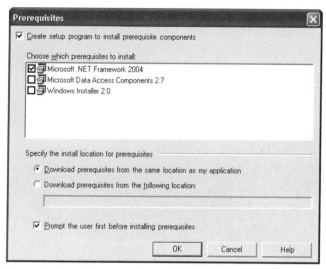

Figure 2-11   Dialog box for specifying the ClickOnce application's update-checking behavior.

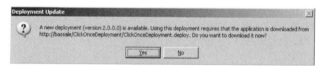

Figure 2-12   Default dialog box offering the choice of installing an update.

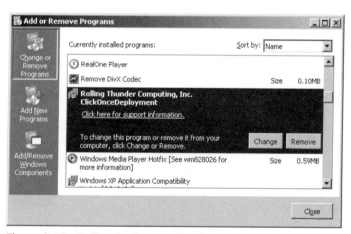

Figure 2-13   Rolling back an update from Control Panel.

You can modify the ClickOnce behavior programmatically.

One of the more useful features of ClickOnce deployment is that all of its features are available programmatically. The user interface that you've seen is a wrapper for objects in the System.DeploymentFramework namespace. The client-side user interface for updates was pretty lame (it will probably change by the time of release), but you can very easily replace it with your own. I did that in the sample program, as I'll show you. The code is shown in Listing 2-9. The class ApplicationUpdateService contains one method called CheckForUpdate and another called Update. As you've probably guessed by now, the former looks to see if there's a more current version and the latter installs it. Each comes in both synchronous and asynchronous flavors because they run over the Internet where latency can be a problem. When you call Check-ForUpdate, it returns either an object of class Version representing the latest version or null if the version you have is current. In the sample program, I offer the user a choice of versions and call Update if she clicks OK. This user interface is pretty simple, but you can see how I'd plug in whatever else I wanted.

Listing 2-9   Code using ClickOnce Deployment API.

```
private void button1_Click(object sender, System.EventArgs e)
{
    // Get the update service

    ApplicationUpdateService svc =
    ApplicationUpdateService.CurrentDeployment;

    // Check to see if there's an update

    Version v = svc.CheckForUpdate();

    // The version will be null if there isn't

    if (v != null)
    {
        // There is a new update. Tell the user which
        // version it is

        Form2 dlg = new Form2();

        dlg.label1.Text = "Current version: " +
            Assembly.GetExecutingAssembly().GetName().
                Version.ToString();
        dlg.label2.Text = "New version: " + v.ToString();

        // If the user clicks OK, then do the update

        if (dlg.ShowDialog() == DialogResult.OK)
        {
            svc.Update();                    }
    }
    else
    {
        MessageBox.Show("Your current version is up-to-date");        }
}
```

Chapter 3
ASP.NET Version 2.0

I've stood in some mighty-mouthed hollow
That's plumb-full of hush to the brim;
I've watched the big, husky sun wallow
In crimson and gold, and grow dim,
Till the moon set the pearly peaks gleaming,
And the stars tumbled out, neck and crop;
And I've thought that I surely was dreaming,
With the peace o' the world piled on top.

— Robert W. Service, *"The Spell of the Yukon,"* stanza 3

Version 1 of ASP.NET was a big hit, but, as with version 1 of anything, omitted many desirable features.

Version 1 of ASP.NET was a big hit. Separating program code from HTML, running on the new robust .NET Framework rather than rickety old COM, and above all the new Web Forms control programming model, led to widespread adoption. But the first release of a major software product is necessarily incomplete. If it wasn't, you'd never get it shipped. The vendor needs to bring it to market as soon as possible to start recouping their development investment, so they do the most important pieces first. Furthermore, developers can't know what users really want until they've actually used the product, or tried to (think Microsoft Bob). ASP.NET version 1 was quite good as far as it went, but it needed many additions before users could think of it as a mature and robust product. What problems did the development team postpone solving until the second iteration, or discover after the first?

Where to Begin

This chapter assumes that you understand ASP.NET version 1. If you aren't familiar with it, I've posted the chapter on it from my book *Introducing Microsoft .NET, Third Edition* on this book's website, *www.microsoftplatformahead.net*, to bring you up to speed.

Developers like ASP.NET's prefabricated infrastructural code and are sorry when they reach its limits.

My clients report that they like ASP.NET so much because of its high level of prefabrication, because it contains code for handling so many repetitive tasks. For example, they love the fact that they don't have to write code that validates the contents of input controls (Were the required fields filled out? Was the phone number format valid?) because ASP.NET provides validator controls that do it. They can concentrate their development effort on their business logic because ASP.NET handles the infrastructural details. It only makes sense that their dissatisfaction with ASP.NET should begin where that prefabrication ends, and they have to start writing their own code to handle what they consider to be repetitive, infrastructural tasks. They want these automated so they can spend their time on their business logic.

Version 1 omitted user and password management features so each website had to develop its own.

The largest omission from Version 1 was any help for managing a website's users. This is a major time sink and security risk at any Internet website and many Intranet sites. Version 1's forms authentication mechanism made it easy to issue cookies containing a user's identity and to use this identity for granting and denying access to pages throughout a user's session. However, it provided almost no support for maintaining the user database required for this architecture. Developers had to write their own code for setting up a database of users and their passwords, and for checking this database when a user tried to log in. They had to write the tools that allowed users to create and modify their own accounts, and administrators to oversee the system and grant various levels of privilege to users or groups of users. They had to write code for setting and resetting passwords, for recovering lost passwords, and for enforcing periodic password changes. They had to spend a lot of time and money not on their business logic, but on writing infrastructural code that duplicated the tasks of every other Web developer in the world because ASP.NET didn't supply it.

We need user management prefabricated for security and economic reasons.

Even worse than wasting time and money, forcing programmers to write their own infrastructure leads to security holes because very few programmers know how to write this type of code correctly. Computer security is a highly specialized skill. The average application programmer knows nothing (or worse, *almost* nothing) about computer security, as a primary care physician knows very little about neurosurgery. The main difference is that your internist usually recognizes this lack and doesn't start drilling holes in your skull when you complain of a headache, whereas the application programmer more often says, "Cool! Where's the manual?" when assigned a security project that he knows nothing about. For example, several developers I know never thought of encrypting their users' passwords in the database that held them to keep a crooked administrator from stealing them just by browsing it. A few others understood the problem but (wrongly, I think) didn't consider it cost-effective to implement on their site. I remember watching Erik Olson's (ASP.NET's main security architect) excellent presentation at Tech Ed 2003, explaining encryption versus hashing versus salted hashing of passwords stored in a database. I sat next to several developers from a particular county sheriff's office, watching them shake their heads wondering how the heck they were going to get all that done without screwing it up and what other problems existed that Erik couldn't fit into a one-hour talk. They shouldn't have to worry about this. We don't need Erik to explain how we should write our own security code, we need him to write the code for us, or direct other specialists in doing so. We want to re-use code developed by experts, not pray that our own bumbling first steps in this nasty new arena don't hurt anybody due to our own ignorance.

Version 1 administration was awful. It needs improving.

Administration of version 1 really stunk. Administrators had to edit an XML file by hand, knowing which elements and attributes to add or modify, making sure to spell and capitalize them correctly. For example, the element reading <authentication mode = "Forms">, with a capital "F," had to be followed by an element reading <forms ...>, with a lower case "f". The error messages that ASP.NET reported when you messed something up (a frequent occurrence) were often cryptic. This level of effort is way beyond the job description or capabilities of most system administrators I know, which means that developers frequently got dragged into editing the files when necessary. A third party, Hunter-Stone, wrote and sold an editor for this purpose, causing administrators to laugh at Microsoft. It was a major step backwards compared to the administrative tools of other Microsoft products, such as COM+, and other parts of .NET. This really needs fixing. We need administration of ASP.NET to be easy for administrators, not barely possible for developers, right out of the box. And we want the administration system to be easily accessed by other computer programs as well, so one program can control the configuration of another.

Website designers need an easier way to provide a common look and feel among all pages in a site.

In addition to these bedrock issues, website architects and programmers also want more prefabrication of the common tasks they encounter during user interface design. The most important principle of Web design is to provide a common look and feel throughout the entire site—the same navigation scheme, the same content layout, the same everything. But that's often difficult and time-consuming to implement, because version 1 didn't provide a prefabricated way to enforce it. You had to place design elements on each page separately and then fiddle to get them just right—Was that border 3 pixels or 4? And when you needed to change your design, perhaps because Vincent Flanders named your site as a particular day's "Daily Sucker" on his site *http://webpagesthatsuck.com* ("Learning good design by looking at bad design"), you had to edit each and every page to change it to your new, hopefully non-sucky, look. We would really like some way of keeping the common look and feel elements in one place and incorporating them by reference into a site's other pages. We'd like this to apply not only to the layout of elements within a page (the links go here, the banner goes there). We'd also like a central location for specifying the aesthetic properties of controls, for example, saying that the foreground color of all buttons shall be a tasteful "charcoal with blue and purple tint."

We'd like to remember a user's data persistently from one visit to the next.

Providing the personalized experience that Web users now demand requires us to remember what a user did on his last visit to our site. One of the main reasons for the success of Amazon.com is that their site remembers what you bought or even looked at the last time you came to the site, and greets you with recommendations based on that memory the next time you visit. To do this, we need an easy way of remembering data persistently from one visit to the next and tying it to a particular user, conceptually similar to a persistent Session collection. Version 1 didn't provide this; we had to write a lot of database code ourselves to make it happen. While the business logic that we'd tie into such a system would obviously vary from one site to another ("That singer whose CD you last bought is coming to your town; click here for tickets" or "Time to schedule your next mammogram, click here for available dates"), the notion of automatically and easily tying persistent data to a particular user has a universal appeal. So we'd like this feature prefabricated into our Web server. And if it could somehow work with users whose names we don't know, that would be even better.

We'd like to allow users to easily customize our website's interface to their liking.

Configuring a Web page layout to a particular user's taste is a topic that a small number of people feel passionately about. Very few users take the trouble of customizing the interfaces of their desktop applications or websites by, say, moving the sports scores from the right of the screen to the left. But the ones who want to and can't get extremely angry. And these users are, by nature, the most interested in your site and the most influential in spreading the word about it, either positive or negative. So, even though they demand services out of proportion to their numbers, it's still sometimes cost-effective to give them what they want, particularly if you can get it without too much trouble. While it's hard to roll a user customization package from scratch, it wouldn't be nearly as hard if ASP.NET were to provide one. And the persistent user data I wished for in the previous paragraph would make it easy to remember each user's settings.

We'd like more and better Web Forms controls, especially for data access.

Web Forms controls were and are a fantastic idea. The only thing wrong with them is that we'd like more. We'd like all the new user interface features we've asked for above, such as user management and personalization, to be available as Web Forms controls because they're easy to program. Most of all, we'd like Web Forms controls to make it easier for us to access data from databases because that's what most website programmers spend most of their time doing.

Web programmers wanted code and HTML separated from each other, but in the same file.

My clients also express wishes and frustrations with the development environment and process itself. While everyone I've ever met liked the fact the ASP.NET code wasn't intermingled with HTML, as it was in the original ASP, not everyone like the fact that code and HTML lived in separate files. Mostly I've found that the system programmers, such as myself, moving over to Web programming liked that, but existing Web programmers moving into ASP.NET didn't. The latter liked the fact that their code was no longer intermingled with HTML, but they wanted it in the same physical file so they didn't have to look in two places for it. And they wanted more of a Web look and feel to their development environment. Of course, changing something so fundamental would alienate the developers who have grown accustomed to it and like it, so we need it to be able to work both ways in order to satisfy both groups.

We'd like to be able to develop without IIS.

Finally, version 1 required Internet Information Server (IIS) for doing any sort of development. Unfortunately, the security policy at many large corporations doesn't allow IIS on individual machines because of the worry over possible security holes. Dealing with the security bureaucracy to get IIS installed so programmers can do their jobs outside of their isolation labs is a needless hassle. While the final production development and testing will still need to be done on IIS, we would like to be able to do as much as possible without it.

Solution Architecture

Version 2 of ASP.NET, release
date unknown, contains
solutions to these problems.

Version 2 of ASP.NET contains solutions to all of these problems. The timeframe for
its release has not been announced at the time of the writing (Q1 2004), which makes
me think that it's over a year away. If it were coming any sooner, they'd at least have
some sort of dates announced, which they then might or might not hit.[1] I wrote the
samples in this chapter using the Whidbey Alpha version that was distributed at the
October 2003 PDC because it's the version that the greatest number of readers either
have or will be able to obtain. I could have gotten a more up-to-date version for this
chapter, but I decided it was more valuable to produce code you have at least some
chance of running and playing with. More than other pieces of the platform described
in this book, the features of version 2 that I describe are subject to change prior to
release. To the extent possible, I'll flag the changes that I know about at the time of
this writing, but others are bound to occur before release.

Version 2 stores its internal
information in a configuration database.

The key to version 2's functionality is the configuration database. The Web.config file
hierarchy still governs the operation of an application (with much better tools for
administering it, as we'll see), but much of its persistent state information (for example, user names and passwords) will live in an external database to which it refers.
The project wizard creates this database as part of the project generation process. The
database can live either in Microsoft Access for small sites (default), or SQL Server for
large ones. As I describe the various new features of version 2, I'll be constantly referring to the fact that this or that piece of information lives in this database.

Version 2 contains full prefabricated support for forms
authentication, including
roles.

Version 2 contains prefabricated support for all the infrastructure necessary for forms
authentication. New administrative tools create tables of user and password information in the aforementioned configuration database. They allow administrators to create and manage users and the groups ("roles") to which they belong. A convenient set
of administrative objects allows you to quickly and easily write code allowing users to
create and manage their own accounts. A handy Web Forms control accesses the database to authenticate the ID and password supplied by a user, thus automating the
login process, and another Web Forms control allows users to retrieve a lost password
by answering an authentication question. The task of implementing forms authentication on your Web server goes from the tedious writing of thousands of lines of code
that you don't really understand and will probably screw up somehow and leave big
holes, to writing almost nothing, understanding that small amount, and probably getting it more or less right. I think it's the biggest advance of the entire software release.
You could muddle through—albeit with reduced functionality—without everything
else I describe in this chapter, but correct, safe user management code is life or death

---

1 Remember Platt's Law of Exponential Estimation Explosion from my previous book, which states simply that "Any software project takes three times as long as your best estimate, even if you apply this law
to it."

for your application or any other application. I demonstrate this functionality in the second example of this chapter.

The administration model of version 2 has changed, and the tools are far better. The architecture is shown schematically in Figure 3-1. An entire new namespace, System.Web.Management, contains classes and methods that manipulate the settings of an ASP.NET application and its configuration database. (Note: the name and contents of this namespace are likely to change in future releases.) A Web-based configuration tool provides a convenient user interface to these objects, allowing administrators to perform their work much more easily. Using this tool for adding a new user is shown in Figure 3-2. Other programs can also easily access these objects. For example, the programmers at a college could easily write a program that checked the external database of currently registered students, added a website account for each one, and removed existing accounts of students no longer registered. The architecture is conceptually similar to the operation of the COM+ catalog, where a series of programmatic objects manipulates the configuration data, and a convenient shell provides human administrators with access to these objects. While many features aren't working in this early version, I demonstrate the user tool in this chapter's second example and the programmatic objects in the third example.

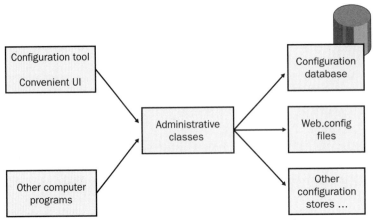

Figure 3-1   Administrative objects and configuration tool.

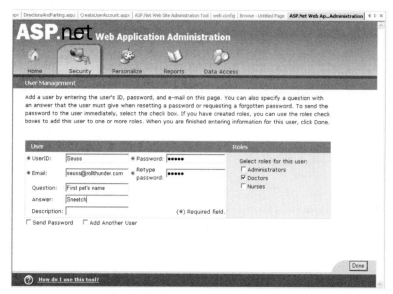

Figure 3-2   Using the configuration tool to add a new user.

Master pages allow for a common look and feel.

For enforcing a common look and feel of elements on a page, version 2 supports *master pages*, as shown in Figure 3-3. A master page is a Web Forms page containing elements that you want to appear on every page, such as your site's navigation structure. The master page contains one (as in this case) or more *content placeholders*, which are Web Forms controls that designate the area on the master layout in which the *content pages* will display their information. A content page is an ordinary .aspx page containing a reference to the master page whose overall appearance it inherits. The content page contains whatever .aspx content (controls, code, HTML, etc.) you'd like to appear in the content placeholder's location. When displayed in a browser, the content page's appearance is the sum of its own content and the elements supplied by its master. In this simple diagram, the master is acting as a simple frame page with a banner and links, but you can make them as sophisticated as you'd care to. The first example in this chapter demonstrates master pages.

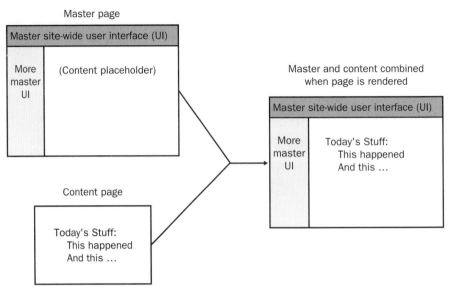

Figure 3-3   Master page architecture.

Themes and skins apply a common set of properties to all controls on a site or page.

Master pages deal with the placement of elements on a page, but they don't directly deal with the appearance of controls. That's the job of themes and skins, new features of version 2. A *skin* is the specification for the appearance of a class of control, saying, for example, that all buttons shall have a foreground color of green, a background color of red, and a font of 12-point Arial. A skin can also specify the appearance of a control with a particular ID value, for example, all buttons with the ID of "btnSubmit" shall have a font of 12-point Arial Bold. A theme is a collection of skins (buttons have such-and-such a set of properties, check boxes have a different but related set, and so on) which are applied as a unit. You can apply themes administratively to an entire site, a folder, or an individual page. You can also apply them programmatically. The last example of this chapter demonstrates themes and skins.

ASP.NET contains functionality that stores user data persistently.

Retaining an individual user's data from one website visit to the next has become much easier with version 2's *personalization* (note that a name change is likely) feature. This allows you to store information in the configuration database in a persistent, type-safe manner and have it automatically associated with the particular user. When your program later requests this information from the database, it will automatically receive the set associated with the user that is currently logged in. If you think of it as a type-safe, persistent Session object, you'll have the right mental model. You can even save data for users whose names you don't know, leading to the curious oxymoron "anonymous personalization." Figure 3-4 shows a schematic diagram of its operation. The fourth sample in this chapter demonstrates personalization. One possible use for personalization is storing a theme selected by a user. (Nomenclature alert: the name "personalization" is a generic term, which could reasonably apply to a number of different features or sets of features, used to designate one specific feature. Beware of confusion unless they change it. "Persistent session" or "persistent per-user data, PEE-pud, sort of like peapod, for short" would be a more descriptive term.)

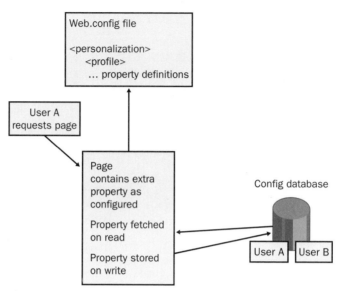

Figure 3-4 Personalization system operation.

Web Parts allow you to customize a user interface.

The Web Parts system addresses the problem of configuring the user interface to the taste of individual users. The Web Parts feature of version 2 allows you to set up little mini-pagelets and allows users to move them around. You store their configuration in the personalization database I described in the previous section. A small percentage of users will absolutely love this, and they're often the most influential ones. I was unable to complete an example of this by the press deadline, but check the sample code that comes with Visual Studio.

Version 2 contains many new and useful controls.

Version 2 contains many more Web Forms controls than previous versions. Some of the new features that I've described, such as forms authentication, provide some of their functionality in the form of Web Forms controls. So does the Web Parts configurability system I just spoke of. In particular, some of the new controls make it much easier to access databases. I demonstrate different types of controls throughout the various examples in this chapter, and the data access controls in the last example.

Code can now reside either in a separate file or in the page's .aspx file.

The code-behind model in version 2 has been changed. Developers can choose to store a page's code either in separate files, as before, or in a separate location in the same .aspx file as the HTML code. Either of them works just fine. When you add a page to your project, you specify which model it will use. You can mix and match different approaches in the same project. The first example shows this feature.

Visual Studio can now run without IIS.

Visual Studio now has the ability to run and debug projects on the individual desktop without requiring the presence of IIS. The first example shows this too.

Simplest Example: Master Site Documents and Navigation

The simplest ASP.NET 2.0 sample program starts here.

As always, I wanted to start by demonstrating the simplest example I could find, but the pieces of ASP.NET hang together in a way that's hard to separate. Instead, I'm building a larger one from the ground up. This website pretends to be Rolling Thunder Hospital, where the corporate motto is, "We help the blind to walk and the lame to see." I'm not sure I'd like to be a patient in this hospital. This section of the chapter discusses the new programming tools, the new form and code model, and the use of a master page to enforce a common look and feel. Subsequent examples will build on the same platform.

I generated a new website with the Whidbey Alpha Visual Studio tool.

I first installed Visual Studio, Whidbey Alpha release. The installation program allows you to select options for how the development tool looks and works. I chose the Web Design look. Once I installed the tool, I ran it, chose New Web Site from the File menu, and chose Empty Web Site from the box shown in Figure 3-5. The difference between this and the ASP.NET Web Site, also shown in Figure 3-5, is that the former contains just one page and the latter contains none at all. I wanted to show you everything from scratch, so I chose the latter. It asks for the location at which I want to place the new site. You can specify an IIS location, or a simple file directory as shown.

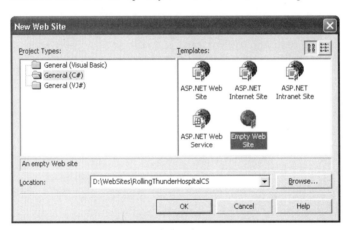

Figure 3-5   Select a project dialog box.

I generated a master page.

The next thing I did was generate a master page to demonstrate the new mechanism for enforcing a common look and feel. Consider the simplest Web Form layout shown previously in Figure 3-3: a banner on top, links on the left, content on the right. I right-clicked the project, chose Add New Item from the project menu, and selected Master Page from the dialog box as shown in Figure 3-6. This generated me a form with the extension .master, in this case "MasterPage.master." Looking at its HTML, shown in Listing 3-1, we see that it contains the outer elements of an HTML page, such as the <HTML> declaration and <body> tag. It also has a ContentPlaceHolder control, which represents the location in which the pages that use this master will place their content. Since I didn't select Code Separation, the master page is self-contained. All the code that I place in it will appear in the master page's file. You can have more than one master page in a website if you want to, and you can even nest one master inside another by reference. But I won't drill down that deeply in this example.

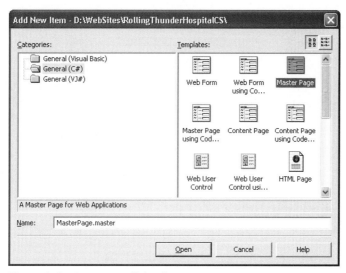

Figure 3-6   Page type dialog box.

Listing 3-1   HTML contents of master page.

```
<%@ master language="C#" %>

<script runat="server">
</script>

<html>
<head runat="server">
    <title>Untitled Page</title>
</head>
<body>
    <form runat="server">
        <asp:contentplaceholder id="ContentPlaceHolder1" runat="server">
        </asp:contentplaceholder>
    </form>
</body>
</html>
```

I customized the look of my master page.

To make a recognizable user interface, I used Visual Studio's main menu to add an HTML table to the master page, containing two rows and two columns. I moved the content place holder into the lower right-hand cell. I then typed the corporate motto into the top right-hand cell. I left the two left-hand cells blank for future use in later examples. You can see the result in Figure 3-7. You can't display a master page on its own in the browser. It's explicitly forbidden, as is the case for a Web.config file. So let's continue and add a content page to it.

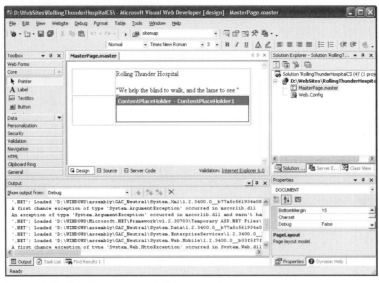

Figure 3-7   Master page containing a table.

Generating a content page prompts the developer to choose a master.

To generate a content page, I selected Add New Item from the context menu and selected Content Page Using Code Separation to demonstrate that feature. I didn't select Web Form, which would have generated a stand-alone page that didn't use a master. When I clicked OK, the wizard asked me to select a Master for the new content page and showed me a list of all the masters in the project, as shown in Figure 3-8. I selected the only one I had. The master that a content page uses is specified in an attribute, as shown in Listing 3-2. It's also available programmatically as a property of the page.

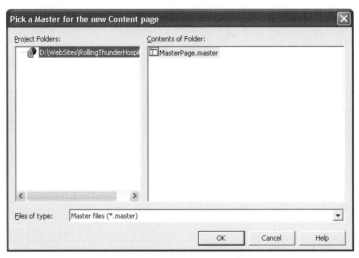

Figure 3-8   Master page selection dialog box.

Listing 3-2   Content page referring to master.

```
<%@ page language="C#" master="~/MasterPage.master" %>
```

Code separation causes separate code and .aspx files to appear in the Solution Explorer.

The wizard generated a new .aspx file and also a new .cs file containing the page's code. The .aspx and .cs files are displayed at the same level in the Solution Explorer, as shown in Figure 3-9. You can see that the .aspx page contains a reference to that code file in its compilewith attribute, as shown in Listing 3-3. The pages now appear separately in the Solution Explorer, so it's easier to open whichever one you want.

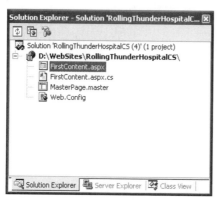

Figure 3-9   Code separation files in Solution Explorer.

Listing 3-3   Code separation page calling out the compilewith class.

```
<%@ page language="C#" master="~/MasterPage.master"
    compilewith="Default.aspx.cs" classname="ASP.Default_aspx" %>
```

I added a content page, specifying a master, and added elements to the content placeholder.

The design view of the content pages now looks like Figure 3-10. The master page content is shown grayed out, so you can see what your new content will look like when combined with it. The gray color effectively signals that you can't edit it from here. The new content page contains a content control, which corresponds to the master's content placeholder. You can add any standard aspx content to the content control on the content page, such as Web Forms controls. In this case, I put one simple label on it and set its text property.

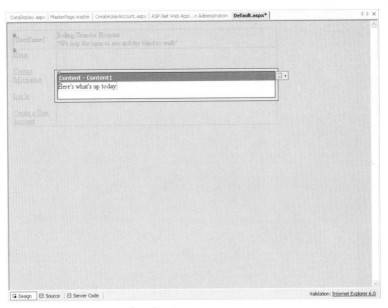

Figure 3-10   Designer showing content page.

Running this application doesn't require IIS.

To check the appearance of my new content page, I selected Debug – Start from the main menu. The page came up as shown in Figure 3-11. You can see the it was launched from the host location localhost:8196. IIS is not required in this scenario.

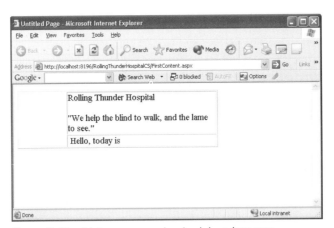

Figure 3-11   Main page running in debug browser.

Page code can live either in the .aspx file or in a separate file.

Finally, I wanted to demonstrate where code would live in this simplest of new scenarios, so I added a page load event handler to both the master page and the content page by double-clicking each one of them. In the master case, which does not use code separation, the handler function gets added to the HTML in a <script> block, as shown in Listing 3-4. You can look at it without the distraction of the other HTML in the screen by switching to the Server Code view at the bottom tab. In the case of the content page, which does use code separation, it appears in the .cs file, as shown in Listing 3-5. The keyword "partial" is a new one, marking the class as being spread across several files. That's why we don't see the full class declaration here, and all of its member variables. It's hidden, but you can see that it's all there by typing **this**. (**Me**. in Visual Basic) and looking at the members list that appears in Intellisense.

Listing 3-4   Master page, without code separation, holding code.

```
<%@ master language="C#" %>

<script runat="server">

    void LinkButton1_Click(object sender, System.EventArgs e)
    {
        System.Web.Security.FormsAuthentication.SignOut ();
        Response.Redirect ("~/default.aspx");

    }


</script>

<html>
```

Listing 3-5   Partial class in page using code separation.

```
public partial class Default_aspx
{
    void Page_Load (object sender, System.EventArgs e)
    {
        Label1.Text = "Here's what's happening on " +
          DateTime.Now.ToLongDateString ();       }

}
```

Security in ASP.NET 2.0

Security is vital to any type of distributed programming and discussions of it are often highly charged with emotion. I will attempt to outline the problems that arise in this area and discuss how version 2 improves the prefabricated functionality that gives you the level of security that you need without too much programming effort.

Authentication

Securely and definitively identifying a user is called authentication.

The first question in any security system is authentication—Who are you and how do I know you really are that person? Authenticating a user usually takes the form of examining some sort of credential presented by the user, sometimes agreed upon directly between the two parties, such as a PIN or password; sometimes issued by a third party that both parties trust, such as a driver's license or passport. If the credentials are satisfactory to the server, the server knows who the user is and can use its internal logic to determine what actions she is allowed to perform. A user who is not authenticated is called an anonymous user. That doesn't necessarily mean that she can't have access to anything on the website. It means that she can have access only to the features that the designers have chosen to make available to anonymous users—perhaps checking an airline schedule but not redeeming a frequent flyer award.

Authentication systems are difficult and expensive to build.

Authentication has historically been the most difficult problem in security design. Most application designers don't want to deal with it because it's so important but so difficult to get right. You need a full-time team of very smart geeks who do nothing but eat, drink, and sleep security because that's what the bad guys have who are trying to crack your website and weasel free first-class upgrades (or worse). For example, you can't just send a password over the network, even if it's encrypted. If the network packet containing an encrypted password doesn't somehow change unpredictably every time you submit it, a bad guy could record it and play it back. That's how I broke into the foreign exchange system of a certain bank whose name you would recognize—fortunately (or not, depending on how you want to look at it) with the bank's permission—under a consulting contract to test their security. They were very proud of their password encryption algorithm, which I never even tried to crack, but it took me only 20 minutes with a packet sniffer to record a user ID/password packet and play it back to enter their server. Too bad I was charging them by the hour. Next time I'll vacation for a billable week before declaring success. If you'd like more information about the design problems of writing secure applications, I recommend the book *Writing Secure Code, Second Edition*, by Michael Howard and David LeBlanc (Microsoft Press, 2003). I never even imagined half the ways to crack a system that these guys discuss.

ASP.NET can use Windows' built-in authentication on an intranet.

Because of the difficulty and importance of authentication, it's one of the first features that gets built into a (hopefully) secure operating system. ASP.NET supports what it calls Windows-based authentication, which basically means delegating the authentication process to IIS, the basic Web server infrastructure on which ASP.NET sits. IIS can be configured to pop up a dialog box on the user's browser and accept a user ID and password. These credentials must match a Windows user account on the domain to which the IIS host belongs. Alternatively, if the client is running Microsoft Internet Explorer 4 or later on a Windows system and not connecting through a proxy, IIS can be configured to use the NTLM or Kerberos authentication systems built into Windows to automatically negotiate a user ID and password based on the user's current logged-in session. Windows authentication works quite well for a Windows-only intranet over which you have full administrative control. For certain classes of installation—say, a large corporation—it's fantastic. Just turn it on and go.

The other alternative is forms authentication. This is shown in Figure 3-12.

But it's much less useful on the wide-open Internet, or even a mixed intranet, where your server wants to be able to talk to any type of system (say, a palmtop) using any type of access (say, not Internet Explorer), and where you don't want to set up a Windows login account for every user. When the user first requests a page from a secure website, he is directed to a form that asks for his ID and password. The Web server matches these against the values it has on file. If they match, the server provides the browser with a cookie that represents its successful login. Think of this cookie as the hand stamp you get at a bar when they check your ID and verify that you really are over 21 years old. It contains the user's identification in an encrypted form. The browser will automatically send this cookie in the request header section of every subsequent page request so that the server knows which authenticated user it comes from. This relay keeps you from having to enter a user ID and password on every form submittal or page request. Figure 3-12 illustrates this process. (Note: Version 2 provides a way of accomplishing this without cookies, by hashing the user's ID into the URL string. The URLs look really ugly, but it gets the job done when cookies are forbidden for religious reasons.)

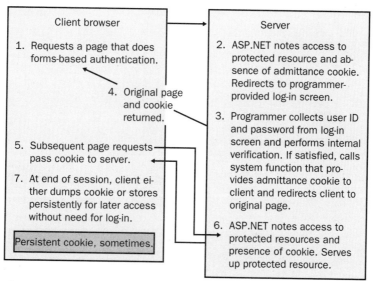

Figure 3-12 Forms-based authentication.

Version 2 now does just about everything for you in forms authentication.

Version 1 provided methods for issuing the cookies and reading them on subsequent accesses, but that's as far as it went. You had to write an awful lot of code to support the system—to set up user accounts, store them in databases, manage their passwords, and look them up when the user came in to authenticate. In version 2, ASP.NET does almost all of it for you with prefabricated classes.

I modified the hospital application to demonstrate forms authentication and user groups.

I modified the hospital sample program from the previous section to demonstrate version 2's support for forms authentication. A hospital website can reasonably have many classes of user, from random surfers-by to security-cleared employees, with different levels of privilege for each. It's easy, as we'll see, to grant or deny access to all pages in a folder based on a user's identity or group membership, to say, for example, that doctors can see the pages in this folder but nurses can't. I decided to demonstrate this by making the top level of my website public. It contains pages such as the login form and create account form, which need to be available to everyone. I then created four subfolders, labeled DoctorsOnly, NursesOnly, DoctorsAndNurses, and Anyone-Authenticated, each of which contains one form intended to be seen only by the specified group. Figure 3-13 shows the Solution Explorer after these additions.

Figure 3-13   Project folders in Solution Explorer.

ASP.NET's administrative wizard can generate databases of users.

Next, I needed to set up my users so I'd have something to test my authentication system with. I ran the ASP.NET configuration tool from Visual Studio's Website menu. This is a version 2 Web application that provides a convenient human interface to objects that manipulate the user database. I selected the Security tab, chose the Security Setup Wizard, and selected Internet access, as shown in Figure 3-14. I then selected the Microsoft Access data store instead of SQL Server so that users could run it without installing the latter program (Figure 3-15). You can also write your own data store provider, implementing a specific set of interfaces, if you need to use a nonstandard database, perhaps a legacy system you can't yet replace. The next screen (Figure 3-16) asked me to select password and user management options.

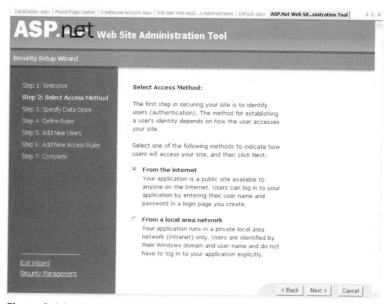

Figure 3-14 Security configuration tool selecting Internet access.

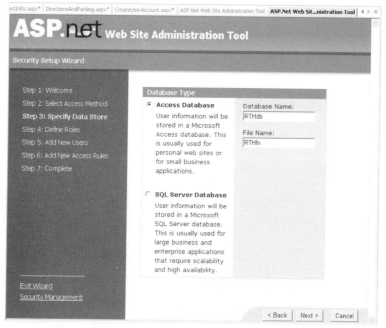

Figure 3-15 Selecting a data source.

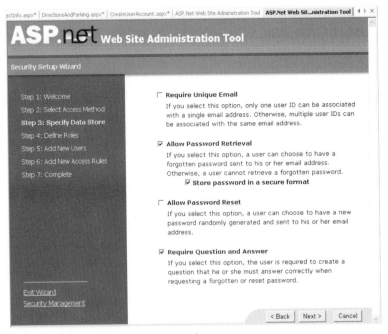

Figure 3-16 Password and user options.

A user can easily use the administrative tool to add users and roles.

Once I created the database, I added some users. Because it simulates a hospital, I added my favorite doctors, Seuss and Kevorkian, and my favorite nurses, Ratched and Houlihan. In this example, I used the user's name as the password. You can see that the tool entered their names and information into the user database, as shown in Figure 3-17, but that the password is encrypted so a crooked administrator can't steal it just by browsing the file. I haven't created any groups yet; that will be the function of the next section of this example.

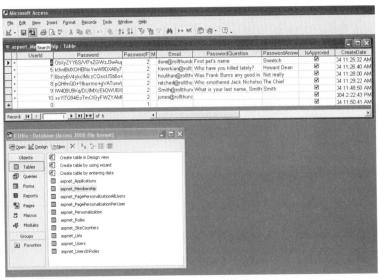

Figure 3-17 Access database containing user information.

I had to make some config file entries to turn on forms authentication.

While it does manage the database of users and roles, the administrative wizard does not yet make entries to the configuration file that tell ASP.NET to use forms authentication. I had to make that entry myself, as shown in Listing 3-6. I expect that the tool will provide this functionality by its final release.

Listing 3-6   Config file for forms authentication.

```
<authentication mode="Forms">
        <forms  name="RollingThunderHospitalCS" loginUrl="Login.aspx"  />
        </authentication>
```

Logging in is easily accomplished with one single control.

Now that I've set up user IDs and passwords, I need to provide a way for users to log in and present their credentials, and for ASP.NET to validate their credentials against the user database. The new Web Forms Log In control seamlessly handles this task. I added a content page called "logon.aspx" and placed a Log In control in its content panel, as shown in Figure 3-18. The Log In control's properties allow extensive configuration options. For example, you can set the User Name label to display a different text string. You can allow (as shown) or remove the Remember Me Next Time box that causes the authentication cookie to be persistent if authentication is successful. The control has many other configuration options, too numerous to list here, but examine the properties box and you'll see them. When the user clicks OK, the Log In control goes to the user database you've set up with the configuration tool (the location is stored in the Web.config file) and compares the password that the user has entered to the stored password. If they match, it issues the authentication cookie I've previously described. If not, it displays a (configurable) failure message. If the user doesn't currently have an account, the left-hand links panel (of which more in the next section) brings up a page that uses the program administrative objects to create a new one. I describe this functionality in the next section of this chapter.

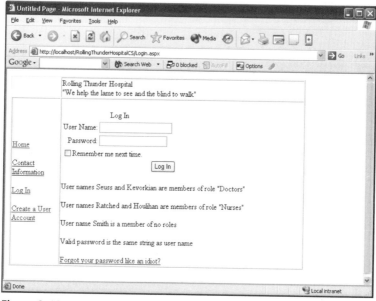

Figure 3-18   Log In form.

Recovering a lost password is likewise simple with just one control.

If the user has forgotten his password, I provide a link to a page containing a PasswordRecovery control, as shown in Figure 3-19. This new Web Forms control checks the database and asks the user the authentication question that he entered when he set up the account, as shown in Figure 3-20. If he answers the question successfully, his password gets sent to him by e-mail. Alternatively, you can configure the database so that it resets the user's password and generates a new random one, instead of providing his old one, which is arguably more secure.

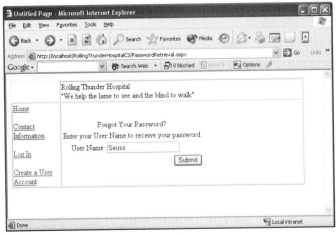

Figure 3-19   Password recovery form.

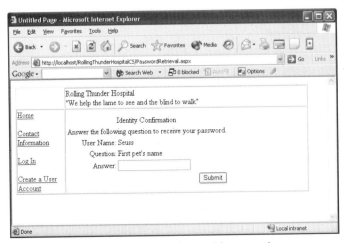

Figure 3-20   Password recovery form with a question.

Version 2 produces a functional member authentication system for almost no code.

That's all I had to do to get my users logged in, securely and easily. It took less code than the example from my previous book, which demonstrated only the method that issued a cookie. For the rest of it, I waved my hands and said, "Your authentication database would go here," and "Maybe look around to see if you can buy administrative tools instead of having to write them," and "Your users will be happier with some form of password recovery, somehow." But now, for less code than that skeletal demo, this one actually works. Sweet.

The LoginName control displays the name of the authenticated user.

The last thing I did was to place a LoginName control in the upper left-hand corner of the master page's table. This is a new Web Forms control that fetches the user's logged in name and displays it to the user. If the user isn't authenticated, then it doesn't display anything. It's a simple beast that scrapes the property User.Identity.Name from the page on which it resides and displays it. You can customize it with its usual designer properties. It's quick, it's easy, it's not too bright, but it makes the user feel like you know her. Figure 3-21 shows this and the controls for the next part of this example. Let's go there now.

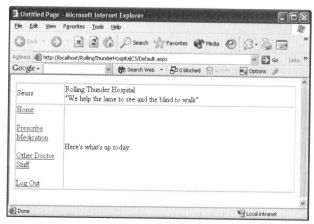

Figure 3-21   Web Browser showing LoginName control and LoginView control.

Authorization

Now that we know who the user is, we can use it for security and for customizing the user interface.

Now that we know who the user is, we can use that information for many purposes on our site. Obviously we can use it to determine whether the user is or isn't allowed to do what she's trying to do, which is called "authorization." But we can also use the authenticated user ID to tailor the user interface to make the user's experience more productive and more pleasant, and thus make our website more attractive than those of our competitors.

Most authorization takes place according to user groups known as roles.

The most important thing I can do once I've authenticated the user is to provide authorization rules that specify who is and who isn't allowed to do what sort of thing. You don't usually deal with individuals, saying, "John is allowed to do this, but Mary isn't." The people involved change too often. More commonly, you create user groups called roles, which correspond to job functions, such as "Doctors" or "Nurses." You assign privileges to roles, for example, saying that only members of the Doctors role can access the form used for prescribing narcotics. You then move individual users into and out of the roles. For example, Mary just passed her doctor of medicine (MD) exam, add her to the role, but John just lost his medical license, so remove him from it.

Roles in Windows authentication map to user groups in the system, but in forms authentication, you have to handle them yourself. In version 1, you had to write your own database of roles, along with all of its maintenance and programming tools. You also had to write your own code to determine at runtime who was or wasn't a member of which role and to place that information into the page system. It wasn't pretty. Fortunately, version 2 contains tools that do all this for you. The administrative tools allow you to specify roles, using the form shown in Figure 3-22 to add roles and the form previously shown in Figure 3-2 to assign users to them. In the sample program, I've set up the roles Doctors and Nurses. I've assigned the users Seuss and Kevorkian to the role Doctors, and Houlihan and Ratched to the role Nurses. I don't have to write any code—none. Simply authenticating against the configuration database automatically fetches the roles to which the user belongs and stores them, encrypted, in the authentication cookie.

Version 2 automatically fetches the roles of authenticated users.

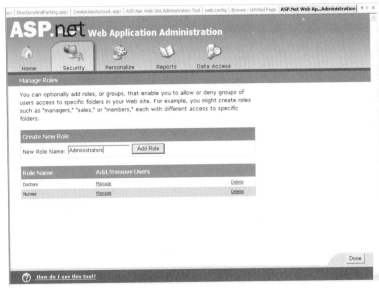

Figure 3-22   Adding roles.

Now that I've specified the roles to which my users belong, I can write rules that specify what members of each role are allowed to do. The administration tool will do this one day, as sort of shown in Figure 3-23. Right now, I have to use a separate Web.config file in each directory, containing the <authorization> element specifying which roles are allowed to see the pages in it, as shown in Listing 3-7. You can apply it to individual pages if you care to. And if you need programmatic access to role membership, the method Page.User.IsInRole will tell you if the authenticated user is a member, so you can write whatever code you want to take advantage of it.

You can specify administratively and programmatically who's allowed to see which page.

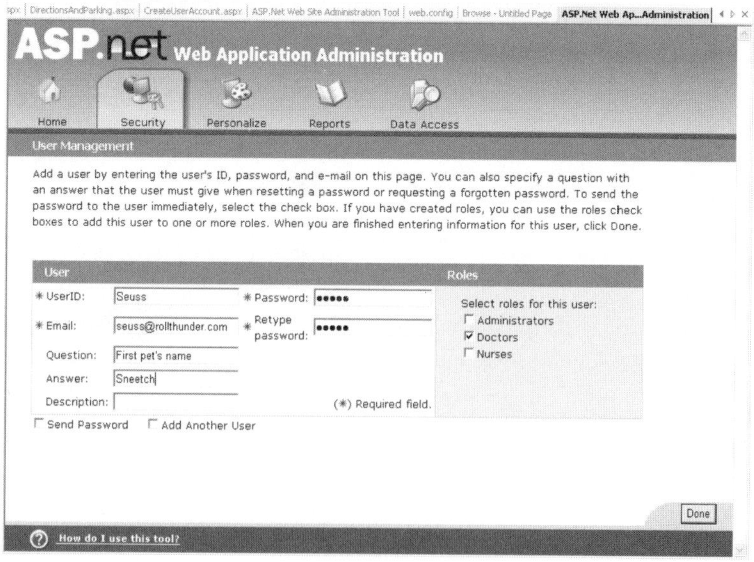

Figure 3-23   Rules page in wizard that doesn't work.

Listing 3-7   Roles authorization.

```
<authorization>
            <allow roles="Doctors" />
            <deny users="*" />
</authorization>
```

The LoginView control can automatically display different HTML content based on a user's identity.

I can also use roles to enhance my user interface customization. I placed a LoginView control in the bottom left-hand table cell of the master page, as shown previously in Figure 3-21. This control exists for the purpose of automatically changing the user interface based on the user's identity. By default, it contains two templates, called AnonymousTemplate and LoggedInTemplate. A template is a set of .aspx content which is displayed or hidden as a unit by another control. Think of it as a sort of mini-pagelet, which you edit with the Visual Studio designer, placing controls and HTML on it as for any other page. The control displays the former template when the user isn't authenticated yet. In this template, I placed links to the pages that an anonymous user would find useful and would be allowed to see, such as the login form, the account creation form, and the hospital's contact information. The control shows the latter when the forms cookie contains the identity of an authenticated user. In this one, I place links to pages such as the Discussion Forum, which only registered users are allowed to see, and to LogOut, which doesn't make any sense if you aren't logged in. You can also add role-specific templates to the LoginView control. In this case, I've added one for Doctors and one for Nurses, each containing a set of links appropriate for a member of that role. The control automatically shows the template that matches the role to which the authenticated user belongs.

Administration—Much Improved

Version 2 has greatly improved administration tools.

The administration of version 2 has greatly improved. Version 2 contains a set of administrative objects that perform the various tasks needed for administration, such as adding and removing users from the database, as shown previously in Figure 3-2. The configuration tool that I've already demonstrated is a convenient front end to allow humans to access these objects. I expect this tool to continue growing and evolving over the months remaining until release. It's especially handy for commercial hosting services, where an administrator can use it to modify the site without having to edit a file and upload it. I've already said everything I want to say about the tool, so this section will devote itself to the underlying object framework.

Creating users is the job of the Membership system.

One of the primary administrative tasks of any system is to manage users. Version 2 does not currently contain a control for creating a new account, although I am told that such a thing will ship with the final product, so I had to write my own code to do that. The form is shown in Figure 3-24. The user enters her desired user ID, password, and other information, and clicks Submit. This invokes the code which you can see in Listing 3-8. The class System.Web.Security.Membership provides access to the membership management system API. The static method CreateUser creates a new user with the specified user ID and password, and returns an object of class Membership-User. You can then use this object to change the password retrieval question and answer, from blank to whatever the user entered. The password is encrypted or hashed in the database according to the administrative settings you made with the wizard when you set up the database, as I've shown previously. The class System.Web.Security.Roles, which I haven't demonstrated, contains methods to create or manage roles, or move users into or out of them.

Listing 3-8   Code for adding a user.

```
void Button1_Click(object sender, System.EventArgs e)
    {
        // If the page has passed all of its validations

        if(Page.IsValid)
        {
            try
            {
                // Create a new user with the specified ID and PW

                MembershipUser user;
                user = Membership.CreateUser (TextBox1.Text, TextBox2.Text,
                    TextBox4.Text);

                // Change the user's password question and answer from
                // blank to the ones specified

                user.ChangePasswordQuestionAndAnswer(TextBox2.Text,
                    TextBox5.Text, TextBox6.Text);
                Membership.UpdateUser(user);
```

```
        // Set the authentication ticket to the user ID

        FormsAuthentication.SetAuthCookie(TextBox1.Text, false);
        Response.Redirect("Default.aspx");

    }
    catch(Exception ex)
    {
        Label7.Text = "The email address you entered is already in
            use. Please choose a different email address.";
    }

    }
}
```

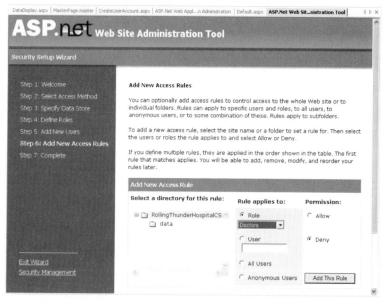

Figure 3-24 Form for adding a user.

Prefabricated classes provide type-safe programmatic access to all application configuration properties.

Configuration properties other than membership are also easy to read and write via the class System.Configuration.Configuration, as shown in Listing 3-9. The static method GetConfigurationForUrl (note that a name change is likely) returns an object of this class describing the configuration of the specified Web URL. Inside it you will find the Web property returns all of the configuration groups having to do with the Web section of the configuration file. In that object, you'll find type-safe objects corresponding to all of the elements that section can contain. This example shows the SessionStateSection, which contains all the information you need about the Web application's session state. You can quickly and easily find anything you want.

Listing 3-9   Reading the session state timeout using administrative objects.

```
Configuration cfg = Configuration.GetConfigurationForUrl
    (Request.ApplicationPath);

            System.Web.Management.SessionStateSection ssc =
                cfg.Web.SessionState  ;
            TimeSpan ts = ssc.Timeout ;
```

Personalization

The Personalization feature allows you to remember per-user information in a persistent, type-safe way.

I spoke earlier of the need to remember user-specific information persistently from one user's visit to her next. The Personalization (Note: name change likely) feature of version 2 allows us to do that very, very easily. Persistent user information gets stored in the configuration database. You will eventually configure it via the configuration tool, but that part of it wasn't working at the time of this writing, so I had to configure it by manually editing the Web.config file. The <personalization> element of the Web.config file contains a <profile> section. In that section, you list properties that you would like ASP.NET to remember persistently on a per user basis. Listing 3-10 shows the config file that specifies one property named LastDrugPrescribed. The default data type, as shown here, is string, but more complex config file entries will allow you to store objects of any serializable type.

Listing 3-10   Config file using personalization.

```
<personalization enabled="true">
  <profile>
    <property name="LastDrugPrescribed" />
  </profile>
</personalization>
```

Personalization data is automatically stored in and fetched from the configuration database.

After saving the file and building the project, you can see that the Page class now contains a property called Profile, and that the Profile object, in turn, contains a type-safe variable for each entry made in the config file. It even shows up in Intellisense, as shown in Figure 3-25. You simply read from it or write to it, and it magically gets fetched from or written to the configuration database. Figure 3-26 shows the data in the configuration database.

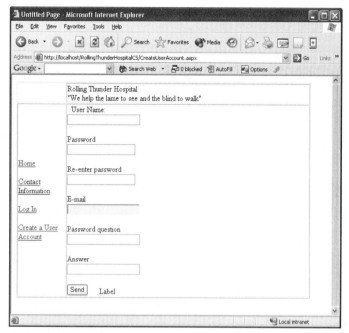

Figure 3-25   IntelliSense showing the personalization property.

Figure 3-26   Personalization data in the configuration database.

You can remember persistent data for anonymous users if you want.

You can, if you want, remember personalization data for users who haven't logged in. For example, you could allow an anonymous user to store intended purchases in a shopping cart and come back a few days later to find these items still there. This process goes by the beautifully oxymoronic name of "anonymous personalization." You would essentially be saying to the user, "I don't know who you are, but I remember what you were doing, and here it is." To do this, you first turn on anonymous identification in the config file, which tags anonymous users with individual IDs. You then need to explicitly configure each personalization property that you want to work with anonymous identification. The main problem with anonymous personalization is that the data can get big quickly because you're storing it for every random surfer-by that uses your site for a few minutes, decides that you're lame, and disappears forever, so you need to write your own way of periodically aging it out.

Data Access

Viewing data with a browser is the main reason you have a PC.

When you dig down into a Web application, you almost always find data access at the heart of it. A user wants to see a bank statement for a certain account, or an airline schedule of flights meeting certain criteria, or the current location and status of a package with a certain tracking number. Accessing and displaying remote data is the main reason that you have a computer today on the Web. Because that's what our applications are doing most of the time, it only makes sense that we'd like to program them to do it as easily as possible.

Most database accesses use the same types of operations over and over.

If you examine data access code from my previous books or anyone else's, you find that doing a database query invariably required writing code to create a connection object and configuring it with a connection string, and then creating an adapter object and configuring it with commands. Once you ran the query, you had to write code to display the results to the user. The data grid control helped with the latter, but you still had to write annoying, repetitive code for such simple operations as sorting and paging.

Data source controls provide easy access to various sources of data.

Version 2 adds new controls that help you to do the database query and enhances the control for displaying the data. The *Data Source* control is a new category of Web Forms control, with no runtime user interface, that provides easy access to a specific type of data source. Each type of data source has its own class of data source control, as shown in Table 3-1.

Table 3-1   Data source control by data source type

Data Source Type	Data Source Control Class (System.Web.UI.WebControls namespace)
DataSet	DataSetDataSource
SQL Server	SqlDataSource
Access	AccessDataSource
Any object	ObjectDataSource
XML Document	XmlDataSource
Site map	SiteMapDataSource

I added and configured AccessDataSource control and a GridView control in my sample.

To demonstrate the functionality of a data source control and the new enhanced grid, I added a page that displays data from the ASP.NET configuration database for this application, as shown in Figure 3-27. Since this database is in Microsoft Access format, I added an AccessDataSource control on the page. I also added a GridView control, the name for the new updated DataGrid, to display the contents. I set the properties of the data source control, in this case specifying the database file that it used and the selection string for querying. I did it manually because the query builder tool wasn't working yet. I set the properties on the grid that told it which data source to display. I also set its properties to allow editing of fields, to allow paging and sorting. I also set the page size to three rows to demonstrate paging.

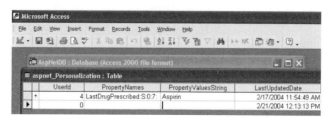

Figure 3-27   Design view with data provider and GridView control.

This data query and display was completely code-free.

When I ran the sample, the data source internally created a database connection and adapter using the properties I had entered in the configuration dialog box, and it performed the query. I didn't have to write any code. The grid control automatically displayed the data according to the properties I had set. Scrolling, paging, and editing were all automatically enabled without my having to write any code. As with the original, there are endless possibilities for customization. And you won't get away with being completely code-free all the time. But accomplishing simple things is now a very simple task, and that's an excellent design.

Themes and Skins

Themes and skins are XML descriptions of control properties.

The theme and skin mechanism is very easy to work with. We'll start with a declarative example. The Whidbey Alpha version comes with two themes, called BasicBlue and SmokeAndGlass. You'll currently find them in the Themes folder, down several levels from your wwwroot\aspnet_client folder. Each contains a file with the extension .skin, containing the skins that describe the appearance of each control. Each skin is an XML element containing the properties of the control as it would appear in an .aspx file. Listing 3-11 shows the LoginName control's skin for the BasicBlue theme, specifying a bold font in tasteful navy blue. Listing 3-12 shows the same control skin from the SmokeAndGlass theme, which sets the color to "charcoal w/blue and purple tint" (looks gray to me) and specifies the typeface and size of the font as well as its bold quality.

Listing 3-11   Skin of LoginName control from BasicBlue theme.

```
<asp:LoginName runat="server" Font-Bold="True"
   ForeColor="#000066"></asp:LoginName>
```

Listing 3-12   Skin of LoginName control from SmokeAndGlass theme.

```
<asp:LoginName   runat="server" ForeColor="#585880" Font-Size=".9em"
   Font-Names="Verdana" Font-Bold="True" />
```

I would expect themes to come from a variety of sources.

While the Whidbey Alpha release ships with only these two themes, you can see that they're relatively easy to write. It hasn't been promised, but I'd be surprised to see the final release ship without several more. I can envision third parties creating many more and posting them for download—how about HotDogStand, which I still miss from Windows 3.1? And I can also see corporate IT departments developing their own themes to enforce their look and feel company-wide.

You can easily apply a theme declaratively in the Web.config file

To apply a theme to an entire site, you specify it in the Web.config file, as shown in Listing 3-13. Figure 3-28 shows the Rolling Thunder Hospital site in BasicBlue, and Figure 3-29 shows it in SmokeAndGlass. You can see that the former is darker and bolder, and the latter uses a different font. You can declaratively apply different themes to different folders of the same site and even different pages, but I purposely won't tell you how because the fundamental purpose of themes is to maintain user interface consistency. I just know that there's someone out there thinking, "Cool! I'll use HotDogStand for my intro page, SouthBeachNeon on my shopping cart, and EmeraldCity on my payment page, and I know my users will LOVE it, because I do." Fie on you! You're probably the same guy that switched word processor fonts every couple of words when you first got a laser printer, making every document you wrote look like a ransom note. Don't inflict your psychoses on the rest of us. That's MY job.

Listing 3-13   Web.config entry for applying a theme to an entire site.

```
<system.web>
   <pages theme="SmokeAndGlass"/>

</system.web>
```

You can easily apply a theme programmatically via the Page.Theme property.

Applying a theme programmatically is likewise easy. The Page class now has a property called Theme, which contains the name of the theme to apply to the page. The only catch is that you have to supply the theme name in the page's PreInit event handler or earlier, because the page mechanism needs this information to set the default properties of the page's controls. I'll show an example in the next paragraph. Setting the theme in a content page also affects the master page to which it belongs.

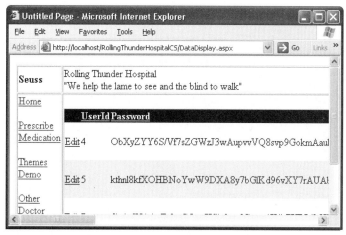

Figure 3-28   Website with the BasicBlue theme applied.

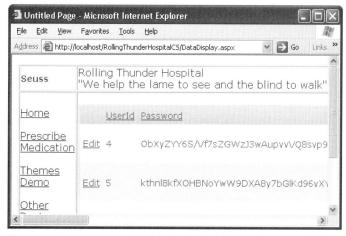

Figure 3-29   Website with the SmokeAndGlass theme applied.

You can easily allow the user to select her own theme for your site.

This naturally raises the question of allowing different users to select different themes for their use of your site. It's not hard to do programmatically. The personalization database is a natural place to store a user's preferred theme name, which we've seen is a simple string. I've added a sample page to my application that allows a user to select a theme from a dropdown list and have it applied immediately, as shown in Figure 3-30. The only tricky part is that when the user selects a theme, she expects to see the results immediately on the returned page. As I mentioned earlier, you need to set the theme name by the end of the page's PreInit event. However, the page's Web Forms controls haven't been initialized at this point; in fact, they haven't even been created. To read the user's selection at this early stage, I had to drop down to the HTML form level and read the value of the user's selection using the Page.Request object. The code is shown in Listing 3-14. The convoluted name of the control comes from the fact that it's embedded in a content placeholder specified by a master page. I discovered the name by looking at the rendered page's HTML source in my browser.

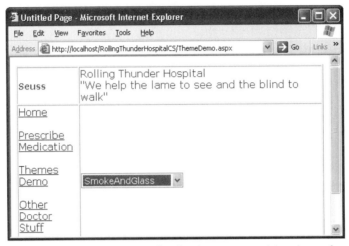

Figure 3-30   Programmatically allowing users to pick a theme for your website.

Listing 3-14   Code for applying a theme programmatically.

```
void Page_PreInit(object sender, System.EventArgs e)
{
    // If this is a postback, then the user has selected a new
    // theme name.

    if (this.IsPostBack)
    {
        // Fetch it from the actual HTML control and store it
        // in the profile database

        this.Profile.ThemeName =
            this.Request["_ctl0$ContentPlaceHolder1$DropDownList1"];

    }

    // Whether or not this is a postback, fetch the stored theme
    // name from the profile database and use it for the page
            this.Theme = this.Profile.ThemeName;

}
```

You can easily write your own skins by using Visual Studio's standard Web Forms designer.

Writing your own themes is likewise easy. Each skin (set of properties for a single control, remember) is an XML element containing the properties of the control as it would appear in an .aspx file. The easiest way to write a skin is to place the control on a Web Form, use the Visual Studio designer to set the properties the way you want them, and then copy the XML from the page into the .skin file. I've done this in the file MyOwnDemoTheme.skin, where I've set the dropdown list to have a background color of red.

ASP.NET looks for themes in a specially named folder.
Your program looks for its themes in a project folder with the reserved name "Themes." Each theme occupies a subfolder under that, the name of the theme being the name of the folder. The current version will recognize only one Themes folder, either yours or the global one I showed earlier. To make my application offer the choice of my theme and the two that come with Visual Studio, I copied the latter into my Themes folder, as shown in Figure 3-31.

Figure 3-31   A Themes folder containing multiple themes.

Chapter 4

Web Services Enhancements (WSE) Version 2.0

The summer—no sweeter was ever;
The sunshiny woods all athrill;
The grayling aleap in the river,
The bighorn asleep on the hill.
The strong life that never knows harness;
The wilds where the caribou call;
The freshness, the freedom, the farness—
O God! how I'm stuck on it all.

— *Robert W. Service, "The Spell of the Yukon," stanza 4*

Problem Background

XML Web services are currently in their infancy.

XML Web services are very much in their infancy today. They provide basic connectivity: you shove bytes into one box and the same bytes magically come out on another box, regardless of the types of the two boxes. In one sense, it's a magnificent accomplishment because no one has managed to pipe bytes between boxes until now without developing an expensive special case for each type of box. But it still falls woefully short of what we need to get useful work done and make money.

XML Web services currently provide only basic connectivity.

The design of XML Web services originated in the late 1990s, those euphoric days of the first Web platinum rush, with the NASDAQ index shooting through 3000 en route to 5000. Marketing types, crazed on their own hot air, turned cartwheels, shouting, "HOORAY! YOUR CELL PHONE WILL GET SPORTS SCORES AND STOCK UPDATES!!!" No one stopped to ask, "Hey, does anyone really care about that except as a short-lived curiosity for sexually frustrated geeks with nothing better to do on a lonely Saturday night?" And no one asked how anyone was going to make any money with it. Most people had the notion that Web content should somehow be free, a hopelessly naive ideology sneered at today as "dot-communism." The open, free-for-all design of XML Web services, with no security or privacy or distributed coordination, reflects that free-love philosophy.

That might have made sense to us five years ago, but it doesn't now.

Today we laugh and groan over our idiocy at the time, just as in our adulthood we wonder how we ever could have believed in Santa Claus and the Easter Bunny. (But we all know that the Tooth Fairy is real, right?) Dot-communism has imploded along with the political kind, as users find that the adjective "free" means, as it always does, "paid for by someone else" (watch a Veteran's Day parade sometime if you don't believe me), and that person usually insists on getting it back one way or another. We realize that having another computer program call ours is at least a semi-intimate transaction, in a way that's qualitatively quite different from having a human view our Web pages. Security is the first thing that any application writer who wants to be successful needs to think about. The giant cross-platform orgy never happened, despite sensuous lubrication with tons of Microsoft snake oil, and the NASDAQ is currently down around 2000. As Charles Dickens wrote at the start of *A Tale of Two Cities*, "It was the best of times, it was the worst of times."[1] And I love them, heart and soul. But maybe that's just me.

This architecture has limited production use of XML Web services mostly to internal applications rather than external.

That doesn't mean that XML Web services have been useless up until now—far from it. They represent the basic solution to a very important and vexing class of problem. But except for curiosity demo projects, my customers report that they are using XML Web services to connect heterogeneous systems within their own enterprises rather than outside them. For example, it's common for an insurance company to have its Web servers on one type of system, its policy issue software on another type, and its accounting and billing software on a third type, and need to tie them together. Meanwhile, the insurance company might acquire another insurer and need to integrate new systems with its own. XML Web services are excellent for crossing these types of platform boundaries. Connecting systems that they control over network wires that they also control is an order of magnitude easier than interoperating with random Internet passers-by, and the financial return much more certain.

We need to address common infrastructural problems at an operating system level.

The situation is similar to raw DCOM on its release in 1996. Making function calls from one Microsoft box to another sounded pretty cool. But we quickly discovered that when we start making calls from one box to another, we encountered new classes of problems which the basic connectivity package doesn't address. These problems include security, transactional integrity, and reliable message delivery; and we needed to solve them before we could make any money. These problems are common to most industrial applications, so it only makes sense to address them at an operating system level rather than have each application vendor spend time and money to roll its own lame and incompatible version. As Microsoft developed Microsoft Transaction Server

---

1   "IT WAS the best of times, it was the worst of times, it was the age of wisdom, it was the age of foolishness, it was the epoch of belief, it was the epoch of incredulity, it was the season of Light, it was the season of Darkness, it was the spring of hope, it was the winter of despair, we had everything before us, we had nothing before us, we were all going direct to Heaven, we were all going direct the other way—in short, the period was so far like the present period, that some of its noisiest authorities insisted on its being received, for good or for evil, in the superlative degree of comparison only."

(MTS) and later COM+ to address these sorts of problems in the COM world, so it is now working on solutions to these problems in the XML Web services world.

For example, the basic Web services package doesn't support authentication, which we need.

For example, any time you develop an application that causes money to change hands, you need to ensure that they're the correct hands. This means you need some way of authenticating users, of making sure that each party really is who it claims to be. This in turn generally involves presentation of some sort of credential, often a user name and shared secret password, which only the correct party would know. The base release of Web services in .NET 1.0 and 1.1, demonstrated in the simplest sample Web service from my book *Introducing Microsoft .NET, Third Edition* (Microsoft Press, 2003), didn't have a standard way of representing authentication credentials in the SOAP packet that carried the function call. You can see what I mean in Listing 4-1.

Listing 4-1   Basic SOAP packet containing non-WSE function call for fetching time. No authentication data is present.

```
<soap:Envelope>
  <soap:Body>
    <GetTime xmlns="http://tempuri.org/">
      <showSeconds>false</showSeconds>
    </GetTime>
  </soap:Body>
</soap:Envelope>
```

Security design is a highly specialized skill, which very few people have.

If we wanted to provide some sort of authentication, we had to design the security architecture ourselves. That's mucho dangerous. Security architecture is a highly specialized skill. Very few developers have the skills and experience to accomplish this properly, without holes, and know that they've done so. Heck, I don't. But at least I know that I don't, which puts me ahead of almost everyone else. And I know enough to realize when I need specialist help, and enough to recognize a specialist's con job when I see it. (Usually.)

We have to roll our own, which is difficult and expensive.

For example, we might pass authentication credentials as parameters to the function call, as shown in Listing 4-2. This seemingly plausible architecture has a number of holes in it. For example, it transmits the password in clear text, which an eavesdropper could steal. It's also inflexible, requiring users to authenticate with a password credential and in no other way—no X509 digital certificates, say, or no tokens of trust from third parties. It's also brittle because the authentication credentials are mixed with the business logic, so every time you change your authentication information you have to change every part of your business logic that touches it, and vice versa. It doesn't scale well either. We have to explain it to every client programmer, and they in turn have to learn every different buggy security architecture used by every misguided Web service developer. And finally, to add injury to insult, we have to pay for developing, debugging, testing, documenting, and supporting this piece of crap. Not good.

Listing 4-2   Soap packet containing authentication credentials as function parameters.

```
<soap:Envelope>
  <soap:Body>
    <GetTime xmlns="http://tempuri.org/">
      <showSeconds>false</showSeconds>
      <userName>me@here.com</userName>
      <password>Fido</password>
    </GetTime>
  </soap:Body>
</soap:Envelope>
```

Convenience and Security: The Balancing Act

Some commercial XML Web services do exactly this. For example, the DOTS GeoPhone service, available at ServiceObjects.com, provides a telephone number when given a street address, at a cost of about 1.5 cents US per call in large quantities. Along with the requested address, the Web method requires a simple license string passed as a parameter to authenticate a valid billing account. While anyone looking with a packet sniffer at the right place at the right time might conceivably steal the license string, the service's designers probably felt that the effort of making it more secure wouldn't be worth the hassle for themselves or their customers. The data itself isn't sensitive, being freely available on many websites and at most public libraries. The value of the Web service, the thing for which the customer is paying, is the convenience of getting the particular desired piece of data into a computer program on demand. Anyone needing commercial quantities of these lookups will find them easier to buy than to steal. That's probably the right level of security for what they're doing, but wouldn't be where larger quantities of money or any sensitive data are involved.

We need a universal XML-based problem domain vocabulary for the infrastructural services.

We need to have these common infrastructural problems solved at an operating system level, but there's a complicating factor we haven't had to deal with before. Since Web services are fundamentally about cooperating with any type of system, Microsoft or not, the design process requires discussion and compromises among many parties to reach agreement on how they ought to work. We need an XML-based problem domain vocabulary that defines the exact syntax used for password authentication and all the other infrastructural services a production application requires. We need it designed properly by people who know what they're doing—the security pieces designed so they can't be hacked, for example. We need the definition to be rigorously written, without ambiguity, so that we have at least a fighting chance of conversing with applications that we didn't develop and aren't intimately familiar with. We want this vocabulary to separate infrastructure from business logic, so they affect each other as little as possible. And we'd like it to be transport independent, so that we can run anywhere, so that we're not dependent on, say, using secure sockets for encryption.

We need a convenient way of producing and consuming this XML-based problem domain vocabulary on our Microsoft systems.

Once we have this XML-based problem domain vocabulary, we need a convenient mechanism for our client applications to produce XML packets that comply with it, and for our server applications to consume them. We want this mechanism to be compatible with the .NET Framework, for example, working well with the garbage collector and other pieces of the Microsoft platform so that we can program it easily and connect it to other pieces of our Microsoft-based infrastructure.

Solution Architecture

We first have to decide who will write the XML problem domain vocabulary for Web services.

Defining the XML problem domain vocabulary is the first order of business. We can't write code to implement it until we know what we're implementing (though I've seen many programmers try valiantly, generally with poor results). And we can't define the vocabulary until we answer Jay Silverheels's classic (but, as far as I can tell, apocryphal) question: "What you mean, 'we', Kemo Sabe?" Who can, and who should, do the work of designing this vocabulary for all of us to use? What does it take to get critical mass?

Microsoft alone can't do it.

Microsoft doesn't have enough clout to establish a Web standard on its own. They tried it with Passport and failed. While it's a convenient standard for single sign-on among the manifold parts of Microsoft, and as such fairly useful, the market has rejected it as a universal authentication standard, apparently because not enough users trusted Microsoft to hold their authentication credentials. Only 83 sites support it for basic authentication, down from 90 a year ago, and 23 of them belong to Microsoft. So we'll need a larger community than that.

Inviting everyone in the whole world to participate doesn't work well either.

The opposite end of the spectrum is to allow anyone in the world who is interested to participate. This leads to design by committee, which invariably takes a long time to produce a bad standard. The logistical hassle of dealing with many participants drags out the schedule, and the participation of people who don't know what they are doing but love to hear themselves speak wastes more time and dilutes the efforts of those who do. The ancient Greek storyteller Aesop wrote a fable about this type of situation called "The Man With Two Sweethearts." [2] The moral is that "Those who seek to please everybody, please nobody." He published it approximately 2600 years ago (just after Biblical prophet Jeremiah, roughly contemporaneous with Zoroaster and Lao-Tzu, just before Buddha and Pythagoras), so the problem isn't new. The latest example of wide-open membership taking a long time to produce bad results is the W3C XSD schema standard, about which the most charitable thing I can say is that everyone I know dislikes it more or less equally, albeit for different reasons. The product of a committee must, by the Second Law of Thermodynamics, be dumber than the dumbest committee member,[3] and that standard is living proof. So inviting everyone in the whole world isn't the best answer either.

The current round of Web services infrastructure standards was developed primarily by Microsoft and IBM together.

As anthropologist Margaret Mead (1901–1978) is credited with writing: "Never doubt that a small group of thoughtful, committed citizens can change the world; indeed, it's the only thing that ever has." The current round of XML Web service standards is being developed primarily by IBM and Microsoft together. A few other vendors were invited to contribute specialist expertise, such as VeriSign and RSA Security on the security parts and BEA Systems, Inc., on distributed transactions, but it's mostly IBM and Microsoft. The teams are small enough to move fast, so they've largely solved that problem. The dumbest team member is five times smarter than me, at least on this kind of project, so they've solved that problem too. The only question is whether these two companies together carry enough clout to swing the market their way, and I think they do. The free market will provide the answer, as it should, and as it always does.

Some of them have been submitted to OASIS to become public standards.

Microsoft and IBM, after designing these standards, have submitted some of them, notably WS-Security, to the Organization for the Advancement of Structured Information Systems (OASIS) for the purpose of becoming public standards. At that time, a number of participants from other organizations became involved with them and will help guide their future development. This is roughly analogous to the progression of the C# language. Originally developed by Microsoft, C# 1.0 was submitted to the international standards organization ECMA to standardize it for future evolution. At this point, I think the additional exposure to a wider audience can help work out kinks in cases never envisioned by the original designers. But the unity of concept provided by a small and committed group of parents will make it much more useful for a whole lot longer than if it had started off public.

---

2 A man had two sweethearts, one older than him and one younger. The younger one didn't want to be seen with an older man, so she plucked out one of his gray hairs every time she saw him. The older one didn't want to be seen with a younger man, so she plucked out one of his non-gray hairs every time she saw him. The man was soon bald, which caused both sweethearts to dump him.

3 Unless, of course, the committee members were maintained at a temperature of absolute zero, which the Third Law of Thermodynamics says they can never reach. Although some of them come close.

You can read these standards online.

Together, the consortium has written a number of specifications all beginning with the characters *WS-*, as in "Web services." You'll find the list on the Microsoft and IBM websites. The most up-to-date list at the time of this writing is at *http://msdn .microsoft.com/webservices/understanding/specs/default.aspx*, but don't be surprised if that changes. Table 4-1 summarizes them.

Table 4-1   Web Service Enhancements Specifications

Name	Description
WS-Addressing	Transport neutral mechanisms to address Web services and messages. Addressing virtualizes the network topology, making multi-hop communication and intermediary support seamless. Like WS-Security, Addressing is a baseline spec that other specs build on top of, including WS-ReliableMessaging and WS-Eventing.
WS-Coordination	Protocols that coordinate the actions of distributed applications.
WS-Discovery	For dynamic announcement and discovery of Web services.
WS-Eventing	Describes a common architecture comprising the necessary protocols, message formats, and interfaces to enable Web services to interact using events.
WS-Inspection	An XML format for assisting in the inspection of a site for available services.
WS-Policy	Describes XML Web services requirements, preferences, and capabilities.
WS-ReliableMessaging	Allows messages to be delivered reliably between distributed applications in the presence of software component, system, or network failures.
WS-Security	Defines security for all XML Web services; contains several sub specifications.
WS-Transaction	Defines coordination types that are used with the extensible coordination framework described in the WS-Coordination specification.

But most application programmers don't have to. Fortunately.

Fortunately, you probably don't have to read these specifications. They're written in computer legalese, which is necessary for specificity but absolute hell for trying to stay awake. They're intended for plumbers, the programmers who create the tools that the rest of us use for putting these services in our applications. Unless this describes you, you probably don't need to crack them at all. Following is some of the legalese used in WS-Addressing, one of the smaller and more understandable standards. Sheesh.

When a message needs to be addressed to the endpoint, the information contained in the endpoint reference is mapped to the message according to a transformation that is dependent on the protocol and data representation used to send the message. Protocol specific mappings (or bindings) will define how the information in the endpoint reference is copied to message and protocol fields. This specification defines the SOAP binding for endpoint references. This mapping MAY be explicitly replaced by other bindings (defined as WSDL bindings or as policies); however, in the absence of an applicable policy stating that a different mapping must be used, the SOAP binding defined here is assumed to apply. To ensure interoperability with a broad range of devices, all conformant implementations MUST support the SOAP binding.

Here's an example of a Web services call using WS-Security.

You can see an example of a SOAP packet that uses WS-Security in Listing 4-3. It shows the same GetTime Web service from the previous two listings, but this time the XML packet contains user ID and password authentication information according to the WS-Security standard. The soap:Envelope element and soap:Body elements are unchanged. But now we're using the soap:Header element to hold infrastructural data, as distinct from the application data that goes in the soap:Body element.

Listing 4-3   SOAP Packet implementing WS-Security.

```
<soap:Envelope>

  <soap:Header>
    <wsse:Security soap:mustUnderstand="1" >
      <wsse:UsernameToken>
        <wsse:Username>me@here.com</wsse:Username>
        <wsse:Password Type="wsse:PasswordText">Fido</wsse:Password>
        <wsse:Nonce>dIPLPzlgHrBMKOu04M5xeQ==</wsse:Nonce>
        <wsu:Created>2003-01-25T17:36:31Z</wsu:Created>
      </wsse:UsernameToken>
    </wsse:Security>
  </soap:Header>

  <soap:Body>
    <GetTime xmlns="http://tempuri.org/">
      <showSeconds>false</showSeconds>
    </GetTime>
  </soap:Body>

</soap:Envelope>
```

The security information is done properly and is separate from the application data.

In this example, the soap:Header contains a Security element. The mustUnderstand attribute tells the receiver that the information in the Security element is so important that, if the receiver doesn't understand what to do with it, it needs to fail the call. Inside the Security element is a UsernameToken element, which contains the user ID and password, along with the time of its creation and a nonce (a unique random string identifying this particular login request). The security information is separate from the business logic. The security design is significantly better (as I'll discuss later in this chapter) and potentially more flexible because it was done by people who knew what they were doing. For example, even though the listing shows a client sending the password in clear text, which would be reasonable when working over an encrypted transport such as Secure Sockets Layer (SSL), the WS-Security standard contains ways to hide the password so as not to require transport level encryption.

Microsoft's Web Services Enhancements download provides pre-fabricated implementation of these Web services protocols.

Specifications without some sort of implementation are useless piles of paper. If you had to write your own implementation of these standards, you'd be programming for years on infrastructure and never get any useful (i.e., paying) application work done. In December of 2002, Microsoft released version 1.0 of the Web Services Enhancements (WSE) for Microsoft .NET, containing early prefabricated support for WS-Security, WS-Attachments, and WS-Routing. Version 2.0 is expected to ship in Q2 of 2004, so it should be out about the time this book gets released. Unless specifically noted otherwise, everything in this chapter applies to Version 2.0. You can download WSE from *http://msdn.microsoft.com/webservices/building/wse/*. WSE is an official, supported Microsoft product that provides security, routing, and attachment support for XML Web services by implementing WS- standards. As you'll see, the WSE does a good job of a) providing a prefabricated implementation of common Web services infrastructure and b) keeping that implementation separate from business logic to the extent possible. Obviously a number of the WS- standards aren't included in the current release, most notably distributed transactions. I hope we see them in a future release.

Read this whole paragraph.

The WSE is implemented primarily as a series of SOAP filters. A SOAP filter is a piece of code that exists for the purpose of modifying a SOAP packet during the process of sending or receiving it, as shown in Figure 4-1. It's common for there to be a chain of filters for different purposes, as shown in Figure 4-2. Each filter is applied in a first-in, last-out sequence, applying its logic to the message. For example, when the input stream reaches the server, it first goes to the TraceInputFilter, which allows us to log it to a file for debugging purposes. It then goes to the SecurityInputFilter, which checks it for the security requirements specified by the server, for example, checking that it contains a user ID and password that match a valid login account. If it passes this filter, it goes to the ReferralInputFilter, which checks to see if the message should be redirected to another party, and so on. If it passes through all of these filters, it bubbles up to the business logic of your Web service. The process is similar for output. The SOAP message from your Web service passes through the filter chain, each adding its contribution to the outgoing packet, as shown in Figure 4-3.

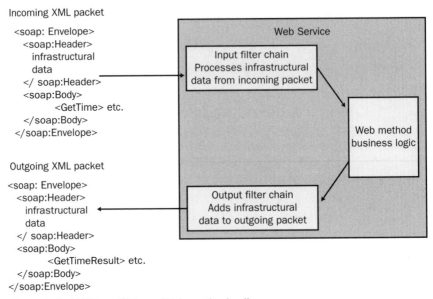

Figure 4-1 WSE modifying a Web method call.

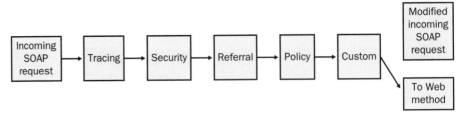

Figure 4-2 SOAP filter chain on input.

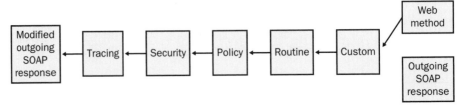

Figure 4-3 SOAP filter chain on output.

The Soap context object provides the connection between application code and the SOAP filters used by the WSE.

Figure 4-4 shows a close-up of the modification process. The filters use an object called the *SOAP context* for communicating to and from the service's or client's business logic, and sometimes to each other. We'll make extensive use of the SOAP context in our application code, as you'll see. A WSE call on the client or server contains two instances of the SOAP context object, one for the request coming in and one for the response going out. For example, in Figure 4-4, the security filter verifies the credentials of the incoming SOAP packet and places the caller's verified identity into the request SOAP context for use by the Web method. The process is conceptually similar on output, as shown in Figure 4-5. The Web method puts information into the response SOAP context object for the use of the output filters. For example, as I'll show in the next section, the Web method can specify the amount of time for which the response message is valid by setting a property called "Time to Live" in the response SOAP context. The security filter fetches this property from the SOAP context and puts the correct information into the output packet.

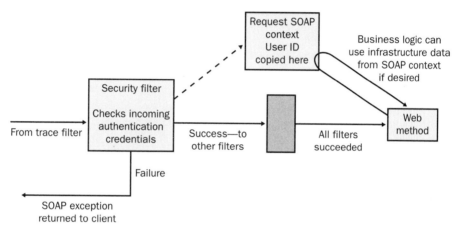

Figure 4-4   SOAP context used for communication from SOAP filter to Web method.

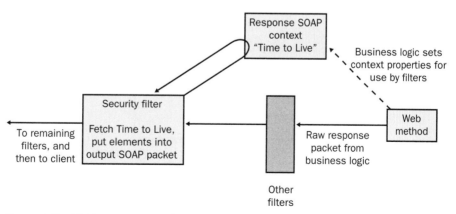

Figure 4-5   SOAP context used for communication from Web method to SOAP filter.

The WSE team asked me to remind you that while WSE provides large amounts of prefabricated implementation functionality, you still need to know what you are doing when making basic architectural decisions. For example, the WSE runtime makes it very easy to authenticate users based on passwords or on X509 certificates, but it doesn't address the question of when you should use one approach versus the other. It provides support for automatically encrypting the data in the SOAP packet if you want it, but it doesn't tell you whether using WSE's encryption or using SSL transport to encrypt the entire conversation would be a better fit for your application, and it doesn't tell you how often you should replace your keys. Despite the fact, or perhaps because of the fact, that WSE makes it so easy to code whichever architecture you choose, it's a very good idea to have a security expert review your design. If your company doesn't have one on staff (maybe even if it does— a second pair of eyes can be helpful), I strongly suggest you go out and buy a few weeks of time from an independent one.

Simplest Example

The simplest Web Services Enhancements example starts here.

As I always do when investigating a new piece of technology, I wrote the simplest example program I could devise to look at its barest bones with a minimum of distraction. You can download the code from the book's website *www.microsoftplatformahead.net* and work along with me. In this case, I started with the simplest XML Web services example from my previous book. The client, shown in Figure 4-6, requests the time from the server and displays it to the user. To demonstrate WSE, it allows the user to specify a timeout interval, after which the request will expire. The server accepts the request and returns the current time in the form of a string, either with or without the seconds digits as requested by the client.

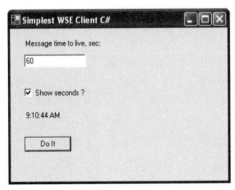

Figure 4-6   Simplest XML Web services client program.

You must install Microsoft.Web.Servcies.DLL in the GAC and add a reference to it in the client's code.

I wrote the original client and server using Microsoft Visual Studio 1.1, but without using any of the WSE. This gives me basic connectivity, as I described in the opening of this chapter. I next downloaded and installed the WSE (remember, always 2.0 in this chapter unless specifically stated otherwise) on my development machine. I did the Visual Studio installation, which contains documentation and developer tools in addition to the WSE runtime files. I decided to make the client program use WSE first. It was very easy using the WSE's configuration editor. I right-clicked on the project in Visual Studio's Solution Explorer and selected WSE Settings 2.0 from the context menu. That brought up the WSE configuration editing tool, shown in Figure 4-7. I selected the check box labeled Enable This Project For Web Services Enhancements, which caused the editor to do two things. First, it added a reference to the WSE's runtime DLL. It's called Microsoft.Web.Services.Dll, version 2.0, and is found in the global assembly cache (GAC). Figure 4-8 shows the Solution Explorer containing a reference to this DLL. All of the prefabricated classes and other code of the WSE live in this DLL. You will have to install it on every machine that wants to use the WSE. Second, it added a configuration file called App.config to my client's project. We'll use this file for entries that control the workings of the WSE, as we'll see throughout this example.

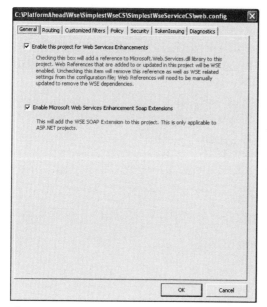

Figure 4-7   WSE configuration editor tool.

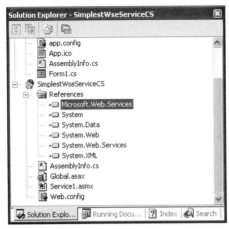

Figure 4-8   Reference to WSE DLL.

I then changed the client-side proxy's base class to use the WSE's enhanced version.

Once I added the WSE to my client-side project, I wanted to set up the filter chain that you've seen previously in Figures 4-1 through 4-3. This was also quite easy. You recall how a pre-WSE client program uses a proxy to access an XML Web service, and that you generate this proxy by adding a Web Reference in Visual Studio. I did exactly the same thing now, but the output was slightly different. Before WSE, adding the Web reference generated a proxy with a base class of System.Web.Services.Protocols.SoapHttpClientProtocol. If you look in the file produced by the proxy generator, you'll still see this class. However, you'll also see that the presence of the WSE DLL reference caused the proxy generator to create another class with the same methods, but using the new WSE proxy base class Microsoft.Web.Services.WebServicesClientProtocol. This base class derives from the aforementioned SoapHttpClientProtocol and automatically adds the Soap context and Soap filter chains that I have discussed. Listing 4-4 shows an example. The name of the new proxy class is always the same as the old one with the characters "Wse" appended. Your client application thus has the choice of WSE or non-WSE proxies.

Listing 4-4   Client-side proxy showing use of new WSE base class.

```
public class Service1Wse :
    Microsoft.Web.Services.WebServicesClientProtocol {
```

Enabling WSE on the server side is done via configuration file entries.

The server side is even easier. For this example, I don't have to change my code in the slightest. All I have to do is to make entries in the Web.config file telling ASP.NET to load the chain of SOAP filters that accomplish the WSE's infrastructural magic. Again, the configuration editor is the easiest way of accomplishing this. You can see these entries in Listing 4-5. You'll note that they refer to the same Microsoft.Web.Services.DLL that the client used. I would also have to add a code reference to this DLL if any of the code in my Web method used it. I'll show this in the next example in this chapter.

Listing 4-5   Config file causing WSE SOAP filter installation on Web services server.

```xml
<?xml version="1.0" encoding="utf-8"?>
<configuration>

    <!-- this section declares the presence of a configuration section
    in this file. -->

    <configSections>
      <section name="microsoft.web.services"
      type="Microsoft.Web.Services.Configuration
          .WebServicesConfiguration,
        Microsoft.Web.Services,
        Version=2.0.0.0, Culture=neutral,
        PublicKeyToken=31bf3856ad364e35" />
    </configSections>

    <!-- This section tells ASP.NET to install and use the SOAP Extensions
    provided by the WSE. -->

    <system.web>
            <webServices>
            <soapExtensionTypes>
                    <add
                type="Microsoft.Web.Services.
                    WebServicesExtension, Microsoft.Web.Services,
                    Version=2.0.0.0, Culture=neutral,
                    PublicKeyToken=31bf3856ad364e35" priority="1"
                    group="0" />
            </soapExtensionTypes>
            </webServices>
    </system.web>

    <!-- Entries describing the web service extensions themselves go in
    this section. This example doesn't have any, but others will. -->

    <microsoft.web.services>

    </microsoft.web.services>

</configuration>
```

You can turn on a tracing filter by making configuration file entries.

When I run the WSE-enabled client against my WSE-enabled server, I still see the same result of retrieving the current time. No differences are evident at the application level, although some must exist deeper down or I've wasted my time and yours here. One of the most important features of any development environment is to be able to look at a running program and see what it's doing. The WSE provides this in the form of a tracing filter, as shown previously in the filter stack diagram in Figures 4-2 and 4-3. This filter logs the input and output packets going to and from a Web service so you can see what the client and server are sending and receiving. You can run tracing on the server side, client side, both, or neither. It's turned off by default, but you can make entries in the configuration file that turn it on. On the server side, you use the same Web.config as for all the other configuration entries. On the client side, you add an App.config file to the project and make the entries in it. The entries are shown in Listing 4-6. The program that's doing the logging needs to have full control over the trace file in order to write it. If it can't open the file, the trace filter doesn't throw an exception; it simply ignores the request. I've found that I need to encode a full path name on the server side to get it to log properly. A simple file name works on the client side. I like to use an extension of .xml for easy viewing of the trace file in Internet Explorer.

Listing 4-6   Config file entries for turning on trace filter.

```
<microsoft.web.services>
    <diagnostics>
       <trace enabled="true" input="InputTrace.xml"
       output="OutputTrace.xml" />
    </diagnostics>
</microsoft.web.services>
```

One of the basic services of the WSE is the timestamp.

The trace file containing the outgoing XML packet sent by the client is shown in Listing 4-7. You can see elements labeled <Action>, <From>, <To>, and <MessageID>, which I won't discuss here. Instead, I'd like to draw your attention to the <Security> element, which contains the <Timestamp> element. This specifies the time at which the message was created and the time at which the client says that the message should no longer be considered valid. These times are expressed in the standard XML date/time format. Note the Z at the end, which stands for "Zulu", meaning Greenwich Mean time zone. I didn't write the code to put these elements in it. They were automatically added by the timestamp output filter in the client-side filter chain, which in turn is set up by the WSE base class that I specified for the client-side proxy. You can see that the default expiration time is 5 minutes after sending.

Listing 4-7   Trace of function packet sent by simplest Web client.

```
<soap:Envelope>
  <soap:Header>
    <wsa:Action>http://tempuri.org/GetTime</wsa:Action>
    <wsa:From>
       <wsa:Address>
            http://schemas.xmlsoap.org/ws/2003/03/addressing/role/anonymous
       </wsa:Address>
    </wsa:From>
    <wsa:MessageID>uuid:5417e299-3e07-4ff1-ba30-bf7e74d3a97b</wsa:MessageID>
    <wsa:To>http://localhost/SimplestWseServiceCS/Service1.asmx</wsa:To>
    <wsse:Security soap:mustUnderstand="1">
```

```
        <wsu:Timestamp wsu:Id="Timestamp-7a0848b9-17de-4b0e-98fa-
        d4c1c634c80b"
                xmlns:wsu="http://schemas.xmlsoap.org/ws/2003/06/utility">
                <wsu:Created>2004-01-22T14:10:43Z</wsu:Created>
                    <wsu:Expires>2004-01-22T14:11:43Z</wsu:Expires>
        </wsu:Timestamp>
      </wsse:Security>     </soap:Header>
    <soap:Body>
      <GetTime xmlns="http://tempuri.org/">
        <ShowSeconds>true</ShowSeconds>
      </GetTime>
      </soap:Body>
    </soap:Envelope>
```

I can modify the default timestamp expiration interval by setting a property of the SOAP context.

Suppose I want to modify that default interval. That's easy to do by setting the property Security.Timestamp.TtlInSeconds ("time-to-live," hereafter TTL) in the client-side SOAP context. Listing 4-8 shows the code for doing that. First, I fetch the request context of the SOAP message by accessing the RequestSoapContext property of the proxy. I then set the TTL property's value to the number of seconds that I want to promise that the message is good for. The SoapContext caches this information for the use of the output security filter. When that filter gets invoked as part of the outgoing call, it looks in the SOAP context and says, "Aha! I was going to give this message a time to live of 5 minutes. But the programmer has placed a different value there, so I'll use that instead." The filter adds that interval to the current time and places that value into the outgoing SOAP packet, as you'll see if you experiment with different values and look in the log file.

Listing 4-8   Client code for simplest example, setting time to live for outgoing packet.

```
private void button1_Click(object sender, System.EventArgs e)
{
  // Create the proxy

  localhost.Service1Wse proxy = new localhost.Service1Wse ( ) ;

  // Set the Soap Context's time-to-live to the
  // number of seconds specified by the user

  proxy.RequestSoapContext.Security.Timestamp.TtlInSeconds =
      Convert.ToInt32(textBox1.Text) ;

  // Make the function call

  label1.Text = proxy.GetTime (checkBox1.Checked) ;

}
```

An expired timestamp is caught by the server, which aborts further processing and sends back an XML packet taking exception.

When the message from the client reaches the server, the server's input security filter gets invoked as part of the normal reception process. The filter compares the expiration time of the message to the current time on the server. If the expiration time has passed, the filter aborts any further processing. It sends back an XML packet containing a SOAP exception, which you can see in Listing 4-9. The client-side SOAP filter chain catches that and throws an actual .NET exception as the result of the Web service call. A try-catch block on the client would handle it, but I've allowed the unhandled exception to halt processing. You can demonstrate this by setting TTL to zero, in which case the created time and expiration time are the same. If the filter determines that the message has not expired, it allows the filter chain processing to continue, eventually working its way up to the Web method on the server side. The Web method programmer can thus be sure that, if the method actually does get called, the timestamp has been checked and has been found not to have expired.

Listing 4-9   Trace file showing exception caused by timestamp expiration.

```
<soap:Body>
 <soap:Fault> <faultcode
  xmlns:code="http://schemas.xmlsoap.org/ws/2003/06/utility">
  code:messageExpired</faultcode>
  <faultstring>Microsoft.Web.Services.Security.Utility.TimestampFault:
  Message Expired at
  Microsoft.Web.Services.Security.Utility.Timestamp.CheckValid() at
  Microsoft.Web.Services.Security.Utility.Timestamp.LoadXml
  (XmlElement element) at
  Microsoft.Web.Services.Security.Utility.Timestamp..ctor
  (XmlElement element) at
  Microsoft.Web.Services.Security.Security.LoadXml(XmlElement element) at
  Microsoft.Web.Services.Security.SecurityInputFilter.ProcessMessage
  (SoapEnvelope envelope) at
  Microsoft.Web.Services.Pipeline.ProcessInputMessage
  (SoapEnvelope envelope) at
  Microsoft.Web.Services.WebServicesExtension.BeforeDeserializeServer
  (SoapServerMessage message)</faultstring>
  <faultactor>http://localhost/SimplestWseServiceCS/Service1.asmx</faultactor>
 </soap:Fault>

</soap:Body>
```

The client and the server are often loosely coupled in an XML Web service.

This code was quite easy to write and demonstrates a lot of prefabricated functionality in the WSE, but I need to point out some of its limitations. The client sends a message with a timestamp, and in this case, the server is paying attention and handling it in a way that the client would consider correct. However, in Web services, the server is often not under your control. The server might not look at the timestamp even though your message says it has to. Or it might allow the function call to proceed even though the expiration time has passed. Conversely, it might reject any message that arrived with less than, say, 10 seconds left on its time to live, figuring that it wouldn't have time to complete processing before the message's expiration time. Or the server's clock might be out of synch with the client's, causing the server to reject messages that the client thinks it has sent in plenty of time. Or the client might be fibbing about the time it sent the message, perhaps to avoid a lateness penalty. (Tell me you've never done this. Liar.) You need to get used to the idea that you're running with counterparties you don't control. It's a much more casual coupling than the intimate connections you got with COM or with .NET Remoting.

The Web service is the XML packets, not the WSE that generates and eats them.

I also need to point out that this example used WSE on both sides. It looks like the SOAP contexts on the client and server are talking to each other, and I invariably get asked the question, "What if the other guy isn't using a SOAP context, or is using a different one?" It's important to understand the XML Web services are nothing more nor less than the exchange of XML packets. The WSE and its SoapContext and filter chains are a convenient way of producing XML packets that conform to the various WS- specifications, no matter what technology the server would later use to digest them. The WSE is likewise a convenient way of processing the incoming XML packets that conform to these specifications, regardless of the technology used to generate them. Neither side knows or cares, or wants to know or wants to care, how the other side is implemented.

More Complex Example: Password Authentication

A user authentication example using an ID and password starts here.

Now that we understand the basic workings of WSE, let's look at a more complex piece of logic: authenticating a user by means of an ID and password. Suppose I want my GetTime Web service to require user authentication so I can check whether the client paid his subscription fees before delivering this valuable service. I'd like to implement authentication with a user ID and a password according to the WS-Security standard. This means that the client has to somehow place the XML elements shown previously in Listing 4-3 into its outgoing SOAP packet, and the server has to somehow read them and use them. It's much easier to program this with the WSE than it was without.

The WSE object Username-Token carries the user's ID and password.

The client first has to place the user name and password information into the SOAP context so that the security output filter can place them into the outgoing XML packet. It does this with a WSE object of class UsernameToken. As you drill deeper into the WSE, you'll see other types of security credentials in other types of tokens, but the UsernameToken is as deep as we're going in this book. The client program, shown in Figure 4-9, captures the user name and password with the user interface that you see. It then constructs an object of class UsernameToken and places it into the SOAP context. The code is shown in Listing 4-10.

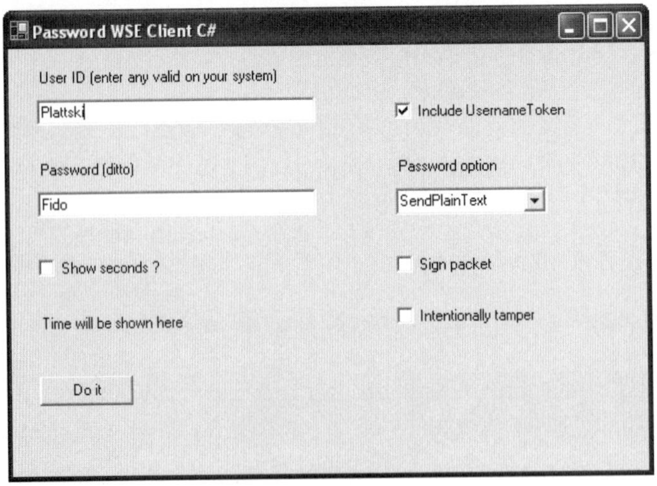

Figure 4-9   Password authentication client.

Listing 4-10   Client-side code for creating and using a UsernameToken.

```csharp
private void button1_Click(object sender, System.EventArgs e)
{
    // Create the proxy

    localhost.Service1Wse proxy = new localhost.Service1Wse ( ) ;

    // Create a UsernameToken with the ID, password, and
    // password transmission option chosen by user

    UsernameToken tok = new UsernameToken (
      textBox1.Text,
      textBox2.Text,
      (PasswordOption) comboBox1.SelectedItem) ;

    // If the user wants to include it, then add the
    // UsernameToken to the outgoing packet

    if (checkBox2.Checked == true)
    {
        proxy.RequestSoapContext.Security.Tokens.Add (tok) ;
    }

    // If the user wants to sign the packet, then create a
    // signature using the UsernameToken and add it

    if (checkBox3.Checked == true)
    {
        Signature sig = new Signature (tok) ;
        proxy.RequestSoapContext.Security.Elements.Add (sig) ;
    }

        // Make call as usual

    label3.Text = proxy.GetTime(checkBox1.Checked) ;
}
```

There are several options for concealing the password in the transmitted XML packet.

The final parameter passed to the UsernameToken's constructor is a flag that specifies how the password is to be encoded in the XML packet. Specifying plain text, as I do here, means that the password will be transmitted in the clear, where an eavesdropper could steal it. So if you choose this option, you will need to use some sort of encryption, such as SSL, at the transport level. You might be doing that anyway if the business logic's data is at all sensitive, in which case this simple approach is probably the right one. I'll discuss the other options later in this section.

The security output filter on the client converts the UsernameToken into output XML.

Once I create the UsernameToken, I place it into the SOAP context's Security.Tokens collection and then make the Web service call as usual. The outgoing security filter takes the UsernameToken out of the SOAP context and places it into the outgoing SOAP packet. The XML produced by this Web service call is shown in Listing 4-11. Inside the Security element, we see the UsernameToken element. We see that it contains the user ID and password that we entered in the client application, and that the password is given in clear text. Again, I must emphasize that, unless you're sending this over an encrypted transport such as SSL, you need to do something else with the password to keep bad guys from stealing it.

Listing 4-11   XML packet using UsernameToken authentication.

```
<wsse:UsernameToken
    wsu:Id="SecurityToken-2c3a916b-0b9a-48e5-8605-5ac8159fd410">

    <wsse:Username>Plattski</wsse:Username>
    <wsse:Password Type="wsse:PasswordText">Fido</wsse:Password>
    <wsse:Nonce>bsdrlPwjduhohaiZuUwfpg==</wsse:Nonce>
    <wsu:Created>2004-01-22T14:06:22Z</wsu:Created>
</wsse:UsernameToken>
```

The server has to match user ID and password with one that it knows about.

The server has to accept the incoming user ID and password, decide if they are good, allow the call to proceed if they are, and fail it if not. The WSE provides reasonable default functionality in the security input filter. If the password is sent in clear text, the filter calls the system API function LogonUser, passing the user name and password that it gets from the UsernameToken, as shown in Figure 4-10. If it fails, an exception gets thrown back to the client. If it succeeds, the identity of the user is placed in the SOAP context and the call allowed to continue. This means that every user has to have a valid Windows account in a location where it's available to the server machine. The beauty of this approach, for small-scale systems, is that you have to write very little code on the client and none on the server. Just make a few configuration file entries, use secure sockets to prevent eavesdropping, and—bang—you're done. Simple things are simple to do, the hallmark of a good design.

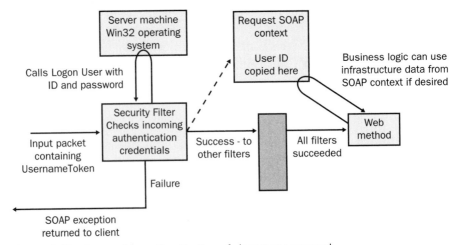

Figure 4-10   Server-side authentication of clear-text password.

The client can send its password hashed for use in an unencrypted transport.

Of course, many architectures will have requirements that preclude using SSL. The whole design philosophy of WSE is to make Web services independent of transport, to successfully run over everything, from SSL to simple e-mail. It is therefore necessary to have some way of securely presenting a user name and password even if the channel isn't encrypted. WSE provides this when I select the SendHashed password option when constructing the UsernameToken. In this case, the client-side proxy calculates an SHA-1 hash of the password, the time at which it was created, and a random number called a *nonce*. It transmits the resulting value as the password, as you can see in Listing 4-12. The hash algorithm is a one-way mashing that a bad guy can't work backwards to deduce the password that it contains.

Listing 4-12   XML packet using SendHashed password option.

```
<wsse:UsernameToken
    wsu:Id="SecurityToken-a913c7db-56eb-4a51-963e-13c61a0aae42">

    <wsse:Username>Plattski</wsse:Username>
    <wsse:Password Type="wsse:PasswordDigest">
        UAUI52sdQ1g1Cgp97XYG7fPRI1Q=
    </wsse:Password>
    <wsse:Nonce>hW4zOfQa+5rNs99SqpUsbw==</wsse:Nonce>
    <wsu:Created>2004-01-22T14:01:48Z</wsu:Created>

</wsse:UsernameToken>
```

You override Authenti-cateToken and return the password you're expecting.

If the password is sent in this hashed form, how can the server determine whether it is correct? Calling LogonUser won't work, as it did in the clear-text password case I just discussed, because that function doesn't know how to handle hashed passwords. In this case, I need to replace the default server-side password handling logic. Fortunately, this is quite easy. The server-side authentication is performed by a WSE class called UsernameTokenManager. You write your own class that derives from this and override the method AuthenticateToken. You then make config file entries that tell the server-side WSE infrastructure to use your derived class instead of its default. The WSE then calls your AuthenticateToken method, passing the UsernameToken. You examine the user name and return the clear text of the password that you would expect from that user. A highly simplified version of this is shown in Listing 4-13. The WSE recalculates the hash and checks whether it matched the hash sent by the client. If it does, the client must have started the hash process with the correct password. He therefore really must be who he says he is, and the authentication is considered successful. Figure 4-11 shows the process schematically.

Listing 4-13   Code for customized UsernameTokenManager.

```
public class MyOwnUsernameTokenManager : UsernameTokenManager
{
    // This method gets called when the server-side security
    // filter needs to authenticate a user. We look at the user
    // name and return the shared secret password we would expect
    // from that person. This example is designed for readability,
    // not production-quality security.

    protected override string AuthenticateToken(UsernameToken tok)
    {
        switch (tok.Username)
        {
            case "Plattski":
                return "Rover" ;
            case "Ivanovich":
                return "Spot" ;
            default:
                return base.AuthenticateToken (tok);
        }
    }
}
```

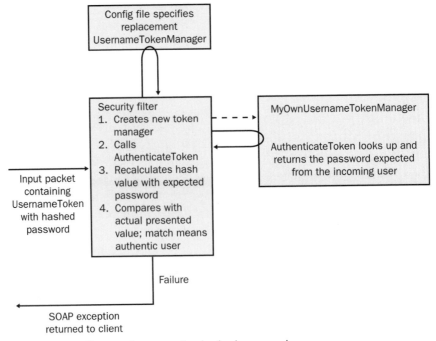

Figure 4-11   Client and server using hashed password.

A random number called a nonce prevents replay attacks.

The UsernameToken XML also contains a nonce. This is a random number, automatically generated by the WSE to identify this particular request packet. It changes every time the UsernameToken is generated. This keeps a bad guy from stealing a successful hashed password and playing it back. You keep a list of the nonces that your Web service has seen to prevent replay attacks. WSE contains an automatic replay cache for this purpose, which you will find discussed in the documentation. Dissecting it is outside the scope of this example.

Many programmers don't like returning passwords.

Many programmers are paranoid about a function that returns a clear-text password to a caller. They worry that a bad guy will hijack that piece of code and use it to steal passwords. You can use the .NET Framework code access security mechanism to minimize this risk. The AuthenticateToken method should only ever be called by the WSE. So you can add a declarative attribute to the method, demanding that its caller have the FullTrust code security attribute, or better yet that the caller be signed by Microsoft's strong name. A bad piece of code won't have that attribute, so the .NET Framework will reject the call. On the other hand, if you have to worry about bad guys injecting their code into such an intimate location of your server, you are probably already, as we say in Boston, "scrod."[4]

_____

4 Scrod, in Boston, is a filet of white fish from a small instance of the cod, haddock, or pollock class. A popular T-shirt for tourists reads "I got scrod at Legal Seafood."

The authenticated user ID is placed in the SOAP context for the server's Web method to read.

Once the Security Input Filter is satisfied with the user's identity, it places the UsernameToken into the SOAP context. For performance reasons it does not impersonate the client. It's entirely up to your business logic to fetch the user's name from there and do whatever it is that you want to with it. You can see the code in Listing 4-14. The sample program fetches the user's name and returns it along with the time string. It also checks to see if the Web service call contained a digital signature, as I discuss in the next section. The functions MyOwnGetFirstUsernameToken and MyOwnGetBodySigned examine those portions of the SOAP context. I don't want to take up the space to show them here, but you can examine them in the sample code.

Listing 4-14   Server-side code fetching UsernameToken from SoapContext.

```
[WebMethod]
public string GetTime (bool ShowSeconds)
{
    // Fetch the Soap context of the current request
    SoapContext ctx = RequestSoapContext.Current ;

    // Check the SoapContext for the presence of a UsernameToken.
    // This would mean that the client has sent a valid user ID
    // and password.

    UsernameToken tok = MyOwnGetFirstUsernameToken (ctx) ;

    // Check for the presence of a Signature on the Body in
    // of the client's request packet.

    bool bBodySigned = MyOwnGetBodySigned (ctx) ;

    // Figure out which time we should return

    string retval ;

    if (ShowSeconds == true)
    {
      retval = DateTime.Now.ToLongTimeString ( ) ;
    }
    else
    {
      retval = DateTime.Now.ToShortTimeString ( ) ;
    }

    // Return the time, along with information as to whether the
    // packet contained a UsernameToken or not, and was signed or not.

    if (tok != null)
    {
      retval = "Hello, " + tok.Username + " , it's now " + retval ;
```

```
    }
    else
    {
      retval = "There is no UsernameToken, but it's now " + retval ;
    }

    return retval + " and request signed is " + bBodySigned.ToString ( ) ;

}
```

Sometimes the server stores the passwords hashed and, thus, can't reconstitute them.

The authentication mechanism shown here works well when the server has access to the client's clear-text password. This doesn't cover the very common case in which the server does not have the clear-text password available. Some security system designs don't store the user's password anywhere, not even encrypted. Instead, they store a hashed version of the password, which can't be reconstituted. An incoming clear-text password is first hashed, and then the hash is compared to the stored hash. This is more secure because the server can't possibly spill beans that it doesn't have. That's how Windows works internally, and that's how some websites choose to work. It is, however, less convenient if you forget your password. In this case, the server can't possibly send the password to you because the server doesn't have it and can't get it. Instead, the server performs some out-of-band authentication (say, asks you a secret question you specified when you set up the account), generates a new random password, and sends it to you by e-mail.

Different websites make different choices on this.

Different websites make different choices on this question. Some come down on the side of security, others on the side of usability. At the time of this writing (Jan 2004), here are some of the sites that do and don't retain the ability to obtain a clear-text password:

Will Return Clear-Text Password	Won't
Staples.com	Amazon.com
Hertz.com	AA.com (American Airlines)
Hilton.com	Delta.com (new password via snail mail only)
Marriott.com	USAir.com
Icelandair.com	Orbitz.com

You can use a password equivalent instead of the actual password.

In this case, you can't get your hands on the clear-text password to return from AuthenticateToken, so you need a different design approach. The client has to somehow generate the hash that the server is expecting to see and pass this "password equivalent" to the WSE runtime instead of the actual password. For example, suppose the server hashed the password with the user ID and stored that result as its password equivalent. You'd have to explain, probably in your client programmer documentation, that the client needed to perform that hash and pass the result as the password inside the UsernameToken, as shown previously in Figure 4-11. It'll work just fine, but it's one more thing to get through the client programmer's head.

What about the performance? You can see that the XML packet is starting to contain an awful lot of infrastructural baggage, dwarfing the payload. And it's only going to get worse when we start doing integrity checking, as I describe in the next section. Won't this knock the stuffing out of performance? It depends on what you're looking for. A payload that is a low percentage of the gross package weight is not unusual in life. For example, the payload of a long-distance aircraft is commonly only 5 percent of its takeoff weight, and air travel is still cost-effective (sort of). XML Web services and the WSE exist for the purpose of crossing arbitrary implementation boundaries, which has never before been possible at any price. They make the tradeoffs that they need to accomplish that goal. As one of my Harvard students once told me, the single greatest performance improvement is from nonworking to working. If you only ever care about one type of platform, then perhaps these aren't the best tradeoffs for your application and XML Web services aren't the right choice for your implementation. But the world seems to me to be moving in the direction of more heterogeneity, not less, which means XML Web services and the WSE will only grow in importance.

Data Integrity: Digital Signatures

We need to protect data against tampering in a Web service.

Sending any function call, indeed, any data, over wires of which you don't control every last centimeter (essentially all wires in existence) opens the risk of tampering. Web services, with their easy-to-read XML encoding, are particularly vulnerable to this. A bad guy could intercept a Web service packet, change critical pieces of it, say, the money transfer destination account number from yours to his, and send it on its way. This is called a "packet forwarding" or "man (sometimes 'monkey')-in-the-middle" attack, as shown in Figure 4-12.

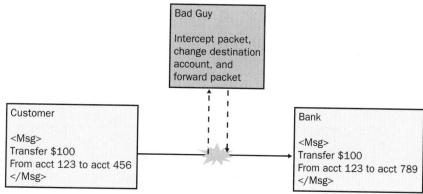

Figure 4-12   Man-in-the-middle attack.

We do that by digitally signing the packet.

To prevent this, we need a way to detect and reject any packet that has been changed after it leaves the sender's program. This means that the sender has to perform some sort of one-way hash algorithm on the packet and transmit the results of this calculation inside the packet as a digital signature. Hashing algorithms use techniques such as modular arithmetic, which are easy to do in a forward direction but impossible to work backwards (think of scrambling an egg). When the recipient receives the packet, he recalculates the hash from the packet's contents and compares it to the transmitted hash. If they don't match, then the recipient knows that the packet has somehow been tampered with (or inadvertently damaged) and can discard it, as shown in Figure 4-13.

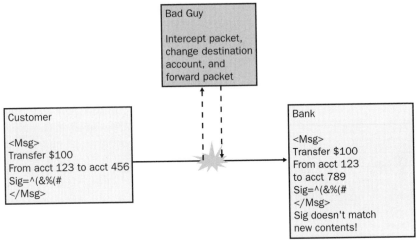

Figure 4-13   Combating man-in-the-middle attack with a digital signature.

You can use a shared secret password as the base of the hash.

But who will guard the guardians? Who will guarantee the integrity of the signature itself? What keeps the bad guy from simply fiddling with the contents, recalculating the hash on the new contents, and forwarding this? The sender has two choices, depending on her relationship with the recipient. If the two parties share a secret, such as a password, the sender can use that secret as the starting value of the hash. A bad guy won't know the secret and, thus, won't be able to calculate a correct hash on the tampered data, as shown in Figure 4-14.

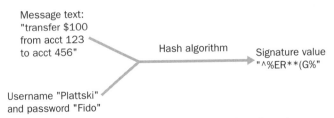

Figure 4-14   Digital signature computed with a shared secret.

Or you can encrypt it with a public key certificate that both sender and recipient trust.

If the two parties don't share a secret, the sender can encrypt the hash value with the private key of an X509 certificate so that it can be decoded with the sender's known public key. A bad guy can calculate the correct hash value of a tampered packet, but he doesn't have the correct private key with which to encrypt the new hash, as shown in Figure 4-15. Since I've already done the background work with UsernameTokens, I'll demonstrate the former technique here.

Figure 4-15   Digital signature encrypted with an X509 certificate.

You sign a packet with the WSE quite easily.

You sign a Web service call by creating an object of class Microsoft.Web.Services.Security.Signature and placing it into the SOAP context of your call. This causes the WSE security filter to calculate a hash value using interesting pieces of the outgoing XML packet and to place that hash into the packet as well. The Signature object constructor requires a security token. The password sample program uses a UsernameToken because it's easiest for beginners to understand what's happening, but the technique works with any WSE security token. The code was shown previously in Listing 4-10.

Portions of the XML packet produced by the proxy are shown in Listing 4-15. Some namespace declarations have been removed for clarity. The default signature mechanism signs these seven sections of the SOAP packet:

SOAP: Body

Timestamp: Created and Expires

Addressing: Action. To, ID, and From

The digital signature XML packet is shown here.

These are the sections that most people care about most of the time. WSE provides a technique for changing this default, but that's not usually necessary unless you add your own custom elements to the SOAP packet.

Listing 4-15   Portions of signed XML packet.

```
<Signature xmlns="http://www.w3.org/2000/09/xmldsig#">
  <SignedInfo>
    <CanonicalizationMethod Algorithm="http://www.w3.org/2001/10/xml-
      exc-c14n#" />
  <SignatureMethod Algorithm="http://www.w3.org/2000/09/xmldsig#hmac-sha1" />
      <Reference URI="#Id-3e8a47bb-bfbf-43b1-b76f-e01fa26eefaa">
  <Transforms>
  <Transform Algorithm="http://www.w3.org/2001/10/xml-exc-c14n#" />
  </Transforms>
  <DigestMethod Algorithm="http://www.w3.org/2000/09/xmldsig#sha1" />
  <DigestValue>PUyfz201uar+c4ui2u+5b2NxdCc=</DigestValue>
  </Reference>
```

```
<Reference URI="#Id-d7cb537e-dc30-4d63-9d5f-9552b7df04de">
 <Transforms>
  <Transform Algorithm="http://www.w3.org/2001/10/xml-exc-c14n#" />
 </Transforms>
 <DigestMethod Algorithm="http://www.w3.org/2000/09/xmldsig#sha1" />
 <DigestValue>TV1zrZRgFKq5LZpy9+H7XjBqgf0=</DigestValue>
 </Reference>

 </SignedInfo>
 <SignatureValue>Ghaa7ObbxDBKKObhdtsSqQW9/zs=</SignatureValue>
<KeyInfo>
<wsse:SecurityTokenReference>
 <wsse:Reference URI="#SecurityToken-2c3a916b-0b9a-48e5-8605-5ac8159fd410"
   ValueType="wsse:UsernameToken" />
</wsse:SecurityTokenReference>
</KeyInfo>
</Signature>
```

You need the password to recalculate the signature on the server side.

On the server side, the security filter detects the presence of a signature. It looks at the items that the signature says it has been calculated from and recalculates it on the same items. If the signature value calculated by the server matches that sent by the client, the server knows that the packet hasn't been tampered with. If it finds that the packet's integrity has been violated for any reason, it throws an exception and never bothers the Web service's business logic. In the case of a packet signed with a UsernameToken, it gets the expected password from the UsernameTokenManager, as described in the previous example, and uses it as the starting value of the signature. This means that signing a packet to verify its integrity also provides you an authentication mechanism. The client can specify a password option of SendNone, which tells the WSE not to send the password in the XML packet at all. The client-side proxy uses the password as the basis for the digital signature but doesn't send the password to the server. If the server-calculated signature, based on the password the server expects from that user, doesn't match what the client sent, either the packet was tampered with or it was signed with the wrong password initially, and it gets rejected in either case.

Simplification: Administrative Control

We'd like to control WSE administratively as much as possible.

One of the cooler features of the WSE is that many of its functions can be performed administratively by making entries in configuration files instead of having to write code for them. For example, in the password authentication example of this chapter, the WSE filter doesn't by default require the presence of a UsernameToken because there are so many other ways in which authentication could be done. It enforces the fact that a token, if present, must be valid, but it doesn't enforce its presence. You can verify this by clearing the Send UsernameToken check box. You'll see that the Web service call still works. The sample service looks for the presence of a UsernameToken in its business logic, and thus detects this sort of problem in this case. But it would be nice to get that out of the way first, and without writing any code.

This example shows a policy requiring a digital signature with a username token.

The Policy input and output filters, shown previously in Figures 4-2 and 4-3, allow you to do this. Suppose I want to make my service require that all requests are signed with a UsernameToken. Ensuring packet integrity is so important to my service that I don't even want to look at a packet that doesn't have it. I make an entry in my configuration file which designates a policy file. The latter is a separate XML-based file that the policy filters read. In that policy file, I make the XML entries that tell the policy filter what to look for and what to do with it. The dialect is quite cryptic, so I won't bore you with a listing of it, but you can find it in the sample code. An easy way to make these policy file entries is the ever-handy WSE configuration editor, shown in Figure 4-16. Here I make the entry to require that incoming packets be signed. (There appears to be no way to require the presence of a UsernameToken without a signature.) The policy filter will now reject messages that arrive without it, as you can see by running the sample code.

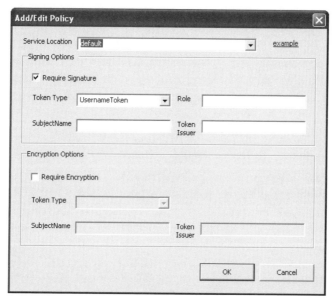

Figure 4-16   Using the configuration editor tool to require username signing.

Policies have many more applications than I can show here.

Policies can work on output as well as input, and on the client as well as the server. For example, I could make a policy file entry on the client requiring that all request packets be encrypted with a public key certificate that I obtain out of band from the server and store on the client machine. The output policy filter would see this requirement, fetch the certificate, and tell the security filter to do that encryption, without requiring me to write code. This would allow an administrator to configure the client program, making it much more flexible and updatable. Almost, but not quite, everything that can be done with code in the WSE can also be done with policies, as you can see from looking at the sample code that comes with the WSE download. I wish I had more time to talk about them. Next book, I guess.

Final Example: Encryption

Real or perceived privacy risks require us to encrypt the data of XML Web services.

The data that you send over an XML Web service is often so sensitive that you don't want an unauthorized person looking at it. Any data involving a macroscopic amount of money falls into this category. Less obvious examples of sensitive data might include medical data keyed to individual patients or educational data keyed to individual students. As a quick rule of thumb, any time you're dealing with data that can be tracked to an identifiable individual, a sizable percentage of your user community will get very angry if they think that someone else might be reading it. Laws and government regulations, such as HIPAA in the United States, may also require the protection of various types of information from unauthorized eyes. In these cases, we need to encrypt our Web service's data to prevent this.

WSE makes encryption relatively easy to program into your application.

Historically, that's been difficult to do because all parties to a communication had to agree on the specific mechanisms for encryption to be used. Developing the WS-Security specification, which describes the XML problem domain vocabulary used for encrypting XML Web service calls, was a monumental accomplishment for the small, dedicated team that I wrote of earlier in this chapter. Once the standard was established, WSE was developed to provide a prefabricated implementation of it, thereby making it relatively easy to program into your application. As with everything else having to do with XML Web services, you have to think about your system's basic architecture, but implementing it is fairly easy once you decide what you want.

A symmetric encryption algorithm uses the same key to encrypt and decrypt a message. Transferring the keys securely is difficult.

The first decision in any type of encryption design is choosing between symmetric and asymmetric algorithms. In the former case, also known as a shared secret algorithm, both sender and recipient share the same secret key, which is used for both encryption and decryption. This type of algorithm can be made as strong as you want, up to and including mathematically provable uncrackable in the case of one-time pads, which you discard after every message.[5] However, all symmetric algorithms share the problem of safely transferring the key from sender to recipient. You can't send it in the clear; a bad guy might be watching. You could encrypt it, but how would you transfer the key for decrypting the encrypted key? Symmetric algorithms work well in low-volume, high-value situations, where you can afford the overhead of sending a courier with a sealed briefcase chained to his wrist to each of your trading partners. In XML Web services, where we need high volume and low unit costs, we can't use them without some help. Version 1 of the WSE provided direct support for symmetric encryption, but the team removed it from version 2 because it's so hard to solve the key exchange problem properly.

---

5   Do not fall into the trap of believing that your system is secure just because you have uncrackable encryption. That's only one part of the overall security problem. As they say in the cryptography business, "If you think crypto is the solution, you don't understand the problem." And as a friend of mine in the government security business once told me, "It's not worth making it cost ten million dollars to crack our network, because for $10,000, the bad guys can bribe the janitors to bring out the contents of our wastebaskets. And for $100,000, they can probably bribe the administrator to give them the password." The cliché that a chain is a strong as its weakest link probably goes back to Aesop. Where's the weakest link in yours?

Asymmetric or public key encryption solves the key exchange problem at the cost of high computation loads.

Asymmetric encryption, also know as public key encryption, solves the key exchange problem. In this type of encryption, the sender uses one key for encrypting the message and the recipient uses a different key used for decrypting it. You randomly select two very large prime numbers (Euclid proved that there are an infinite number of them) and multiply them together. The product is your public key and the two separate factors are your private key. You publish the former (post it on your website, write it on your business card, take out a full-page ad in the New York Times) but keep the latter secret. It never leaves your site. Anyone wanting to send you a message encrypts it with your public key. A bad guy who intercepts the message has your public key, but he can't use it to decrypt the message. He needs the two prime factors, and it's very hard to work backward to them from the product. You, on the other hand, have the private key containing those two factors, so you can decrypt it with relative ease. The only drawback to this type of algorithm is that it takes a great deal of computing power, roughly 1000 times as much as a symmetric algorithm. Anyone who is interested will find the mathematics of asymmetric encryption, as well as a fascinating discussion of its development and all things cryptographic, in *The Code Book* by Simon Singh (Anchor, 2000).

Many modern-day cryptographic schemes combine the two types of algorithms.

Many modern-day cryptographic schemes, such as Secure Sockets and Pretty Good Privacy, combine the two types of algorithms. When you want send a message, you generate a new random symmetric key and encrypt the message with it. You then get the recipient's public (asymmetric) key, encrypt the symmetric key with that, and send both message and key to the recipient. The recipient decrypts the symmetric key with her private key, and then uses that symmetric key to decrypt the message. It's more efficient because the long messages are encrypted with the cheaper symmetric algorithm, while the more expensive public key algorithm is used only for securely exchanging the symmetric keys. The next message will use a different symmetric key, making it much harder for bad guys to crack them by placing the messages in depth.

WSE uses a combination of algorithm types as well.

WSE also uses a combination of symmetric and asymmetric algorithms to support encryption. The most basic form uses public keys in the form of X509 certificates, but you can write your own security token class if you need to get them from somewhere else. I won't address the issue of how you get these from recipient to sender. Because your public key is by definition public, any logistically convenient mechanism, such as the ordinary e-mail you might use in setting up a client account with the XML Web service, is fine. Or you might design the Web service itself to expose a method for fetching its public key.

It's easy to tell WSE to encrypt the data.

I've written a sample program to demonstrate the encryption features of WSE. The client program is shown in Figure 4-17. It requires the X509 sample certificates that shipped with the WSE samples to be installed on the machine. The code is shown in Listing 4-16. The client program uses a private function (I won't bore you with it here, but it's in the sample code) to read the server's public key certificate out of the client machine's certificate store and creates an X509 security token with it. The client then creates a new object of class EncryptedData based on this token, which tells the WSE's output security filters to encrypt the data using the public key in the token. Finally, the client places the EncryptedData object into the request SOAP context where the filters will find it. As the message sending process takes place, the WSE's output security filter looks in the SOAP context, sees that it has been told to encrypt with that key, and does so. As I said, it's pretty easy to program. And in fact, the same administrative shortcut that I wrote about in the preceding section will work here as well, if you'd rather do it administratively.

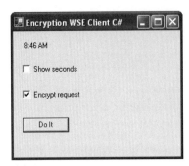

Figure 4-17   WSE client program.

Listing 4-16   Code of client encrypting message to server.

```
private void button1_Click(object sender, System.EventArgs e)
    {
        // Create proxy as usual

        localhost.Service1Wse proxy = new localhost.Service1Wse ( ) ;

        if (checkBox2.Checked == true)
        {
            // Get X509 certificate containing recipient's public key

            X509Certificate cert = MyOwnGetX509Certificate ( )  ;

            // Create a token based on that certificate.

            X509SecurityToken token = new X509SecurityToken (cert) ;

            // Create the EncryptedData object based on that certificate

            EncryptedData enc = new EncryptedData(token)  ;

            // Add the EncryptedData to the SOAP packet

            proxy.RequestSoapContext.Security.Elements.Add (enc) ;

        }
```

The server-side security filter automatically decrypts the message.

On the server side, the input-side security filter sees that the incoming packet has been encrypted. It automatically fetches the required private key from the server's X509 certificate store and uses it to start the decryption process. If the decryption is successful, the server-side Web method gets called, and if not, it throws an exception.

The SOAP:Body contains encrypted data.

The SOAP:Body element of the packet sent by the client, heavily excerpted for clarity, is shown in Listing 4-17. Instead of GetTime and ShowSeconds, we see an element called EncryptedData. This contains the method name and its parameters, but encrypted so an eavesdropper can't see them. Note that it has an attribute called "Id," which we'll come back to in the next paragraph. Inside the EncryptedData, we see an EncryptionMethod element, with an Algorithm attribute that ends with the characters "aes128-cbc". This is the name of a strong and modern symmetrical encryption algorithm, which the WSE has used to encrypt the data. We also see the CipherData and CipherValue blocks, which contain the actual encrypted data. Even though we gave the SOAP context an asymmetric public key, it has encrypted our method call with a symmetrical algorithm for efficiency. Fine, but now how can the recipient decrypt it?

Listing 4-17   Encrypted packet body.

```
<soap:Body>
        <xenc:EncryptedData
          Id="EncryptedContent-01e27e0b-0898-4361-bbcb-06c54ecec4c3" >
                <xenc:EncryptionMethod
                  Algorithm="http://www.w3.org/2001/04/xmlenc#aes128-cbc" />
                <xenc:CipherData>
                        <xenc:CipherValue>
                                jkNXbjzO2VVOVu5AziGL/ …
                        </xenc:CipherValue>
                </xenc:CipherData>
        </xenc:EncryptedData>
</soap:Body>
```

The key itself is encrypted in a public key algorithm and placed in the SOAP:Header element.

Listing 4-18 shows an excerpt from the Security section of the same packet's SOAP:Header element. This contains the symmetric key used to encrypt the SOAP:Body, encrypted with the server's public key so a bad guy can't steal it. It has an EncryptedKey element, encrypted with an algorithm ending in the characters "rsa-1_5". This is the standard asymmetrical algorithm named after its inventors, Rivest, Shamir, and Adelman. The KeyInfo element tells the recipient that the private key for decrypting it can be found in the X509 certificate whose value is identified by the string starting with "bBwP". Looking at the rest of the packet, you see the CipherData and CipherValue containing the encrypted value of the symmetric key. The ReferenceList element contains one DataReference element for each section of the packet encrypted with the symmetric key. This tells the recipient's security filter which section of the incoming packet to decrypt with the symmetric key, once they've decrypted the key itself. In this case, there is only one, which you can see has the same value as the "Id" attribute we saw in the SOAP:Body.

Listing 4-18   SOAP output packet showing encrypted method call.

```
<xenc:EncryptedKey>
      <xenc:EncryptionMethod
        Algorithm="http://www.w3.org/2001/04/xmlenc#rsa-1_5" />
      <KeyInfo xmlns="http://www.w3.org/2000/09/xmldsig#">
            <wsse:SecurityTokenReference>
                  <wsse:KeyIdentifier ValueType="wsse:X509v3">
                        bBwPfItvKp3b6TNDq+14qs58VJQ=
                  </wsse:KeyIdentifier>
            </wsse:SecurityTokenReference>
      </KeyInfo>
      <xenc:CipherData>
            <xenc:CipherValue>
                  HmKwtHHETtJ …
            </xenc:CipherValue>
      </xenc:CipherData>
      <xenc:ReferenceList>
            <xenc:DataReference
                URI="#EncryptedContent-01e27e0b-0898-4361-bbcb-
            06c54ecec4c3" />
      </xenc:ReferenceList>
</xenc:EncryptedKey>

<xenc:EncryptedKey>
      <xenc:EncryptionMethod
            Algorithm="http://www.w3.org/2001/04/xmlenc#rsa-1_5" />
      <KeyInfo>
            <wsse:SecurityTokenReference>
                  <wsse:KeyIdentifier ValueType="wsse:X509v3">
                        bBwPfItvKp3b6TNDq+14qs58VJQ=
                  </wsse:KeyIdentifier>
            </wsse:SecurityTokenReference>
      </KeyInfo>

      <xenc:CipherData>
            <xenc:CipherValue>

                  (omitted)

            </xenc:CipherValue>
      </xenc:CipherData>
      <xenc:ReferenceList>
                  <xenc:DataReference
                        URI="#EncryptedContent-01e27e0b-0898-4361-bbcb-
                  06c54ecec4c3" />
      </xenc:ReferenceList>
</xenc:EncryptedKey>
```

WSE has many other encryption capabilities than I can
list here.

WSE has many more capabilities for encryption than I have time to list here. For example, by default it encrypts only the Body section of the SOAP packet, but you can tell it to encrypt other parts as well, perhaps a password if you're using that for authentication. You can use the Trusted Conversation service to negotiate a symmetric encryption key once and use it for multiple calls over some period of time, thus saving the overhead of generating and encrypting the symmetric key on every call. You can also use the public key mechanism for authentication instead of the passwords I've shown. If recipients can decrypt a message or signature with the public key that they know is yours, then they know it must have been encrypted with your private key and, therefore, it must really come from you.

Chapter 5
Microsoft .NET Compact Framework, Smartphone, and MapPoint Web Service

The winter! the brightness that blinds you,
*   The white land locked tight as a drum,*
The cold fear that follows and finds you,
*   The silence that bludgeons you dumb.*
The snows that are older than history,
*   The woods where the weird shadows slant;*
The stillness, the moonlight, the mystery,
*   I've bade 'em good-by – but I can't.*

– Robert W. Service, "The Spell of the Yukon," stanza 5

Problem Background

The PC market is saturated. Most of the software you've written, and I've written about, is meant to run on generic personal computers. PCs have already penetrated to almost every place they can ever occupy. There aren't many desktops that could accept a PC that don't already have one. That doesn't mean that there isn't a place for new PC software, but it does mean that opportunities for the explosive growth to which the software industry has become accustomed won't and can't continue to happen on that platform.

PCs are inherently generic devices. The whole point of a PC is that its generic hardware and operating system allow it to do anything by running different application software—manage personal finances, download pornography, compose a symphony. Precisely because it can do all of these things, it doesn't do any of them particularly well. It can't be optimized for any one task, as it has to remain capable of all the others.

Déjà Vu

We've seen this situation before, about 100 years ago with electric motors, and solved it when they got cheap enough to multiply, dedicate, and optimize.

The situation today, with Internet access primarily available through a generic browser program on a generic PC box, is similar to the early part of the twentieth century when electricity first started arriving in United States households. Electric motors weren't usually built into household appliances then. Sears sold a stand-alone electric motor (for $8.75 US) that you could connect to different appliances, such as your sewing machine, mixer, or fan. You had to connect and configure the motor before you could use the appliance. You could probably afford only one motor, so you had to choose between sewing and fanning if your clothes needed mending on a hot day. You probably only had one or two electric outlets to plug it into. And since the motor had to run with all kinds of different appliances, it didn't serve any of them particularly well. As motors got smaller and cheaper, they were built into individual appliances to the point that it's difficult today to buy a toothbrush or a carving knife that doesn't contain at least one motor. Modern appliances are easy to use because the motor and its infrastructure (power supply, linkages, and so on) are optimized for each specific task and hidden from you. You can plug it in almost anywhere, and many battery-powered devices don't require wires at all. You don't think about the motors; you just turn your appliance on and use its dedicated human interface.

Internet access will soon be baked into every electronic device, just as motors are.

The same sort of seismic shift is just now beginning in Internet programming. Just as motors were built into appliances, so Internet access will soon be built directly into every electronic device that anyone builds. You won't use a generic browser on a PC except when generic browsing is what you feel like doing. Instead, each device will use the Internet in a way tailored for accomplishing its own specific tasks and mediated by its own specific user interface. You won't think about the device's Internet access, just as you don't think about the motors in your appliances (except when they break, and the same will apply to dedicated Internet devices).

Here's an example in a commercially available bookshelf stereo system.

Consider, for example, the Philips MCi250 Wireless Broadband Internet Micro HiFi System that is available today for $280 US from Amazon.com and looks like a standard bookshelf stereo system. But unlike others, it contains a wireless broadband connection that lets it play music streams from the Internet. Caribbean music addicts such as myself can tune in to Jimmy Buffet and friends 24 hours a day on *RadioMargaritaville.com* or, if that's down, on *CoveRunner.com*. We don't think about the Internet technology that delivers the stream. It just shows up on the box as does an AM or FM station—two other technologies that we've long since stopped thinking about as well. (Do you even know what they stand for?)[1] It's not hard to imagine a day when Internet streaming is a standard feature of every music system anyone sells. And they'll all require software, good software, in the showroom to make the sale and then in the living room to play music for the user. Now think about TV. Now think about cars. Ubiquitous connectivity has been coming for a long time. The falling cost of it is about to make the market explode.

Mobile devices are another class of smart device.

A special class of these sub-PC intelligent devices are the mobile computing devices, such as the Pocket PC and the Smartphone. Their main attraction is the easy portability of their computing power. These devices also require good software. But the mobility of the devices dictates that we develop different types of software than for their sessile[2] cousins.

Palmtop devices haven't caught on with the general public yet.

The Pocket PC is the Microsoft-specific name for a palmtop computing device. The boxes are roughly the size of your hand, as shown in Figure 5-1, hence the brand name, and also the generic name "palmtop." As with desktop PCs, hardware manufacturers such as Dell and HP produce the hardware and Microsoft produces the operating system software. Microsoft promotes these appliances as general purpose computing devices similar to a PC, as the name "Pocket PC" and the presence of Pocket Word and Pocket Excel indicate. But the palmtop computing genre hasn't yet caught on with the general public to anywhere near the degree that the PC or "dumb" cell phone have. I polled several of my classes in late 2003 and found that ownership of any palmtop ranged from 5 percent in Wisconsin to 10 percent in Boston and 20 percent in New York City (where users reported that the small form factor made them convenient on cramped train commutes). Microsoft operating systems accounted for roughly one third of these systems, the remainder being Palm OS from PalmSource, Inc. The attendees were all programmers learning Microsoft .NET, whom you would expect to be the most savvy, technophilic, and Microsoft-centric people alive. Very few users are currently saying with their money that they find a palmtop's portability to be worth the difficulty of doing any sort of text input on them, or of reading from the small screen, or of lugging around another box about three times the size of their cell phones. The next time you take a plane trip, walk up and down the aisle and see what the passengers are using. You'll see a lot of notebook PCs, many CD players and portable music players, a few dedicated DVD players, but not many palmtops.

---

1 AM stands for "amplitude modulation," which means that the audio signal is encoded in the height of the radio carrier wave. FM stands for "frequency modulation," which means that the audio signal is encoded in the distance between peaks of the radio carrier wave. While it doesn't seem to have grown popular yet, I've seen the term "IM" used to describe audio signals delivered over the Internet, precisely to encourage this form of familiarity.

2 This means permanently attached or fixed in location. A barnacle, like a desktop PC, is sessile. A fish, like a Pocket PC, is not.

Figure 5-1 Pocket PC form factor.

We need to start thinking of them as computing devices in their own right, not lame but portable PCs.

To my mind, the slow adoption of palmtop devices stems from a fundamental misunderstanding of a) their capabilities and benefits, and b) the needs of real people. Always remember that, unless you are writing programs for burned-out computer geeks, your user is not you. What you value is not necessarily what your user values. How many of you readers bother putting your daily task list on any computer at all? Less than a quarter, I guarantee it. And how many of you bother to transfer them to a smart device you carry with you? Fewer still, and you're the ones who love technology for its own sake. I find that a paper index card works better for both applications. And you're (OK, we're) all geeks. If we don't do it, what about the general public, the great masses who have our money in their pockets, whence we somehow need to extract it? That's not what they care about. However, once you stop thinking of Pocket PCs and Smartphones as general computing devices, clear your mind and ask yourself, "Just what annoying real-world problems could such a device solve?", you'll see at least two big ones.

A prize-winning application used Pocket PCs as bilingual order entry devices for waiters in an ethnic restaurant.

The first is the problem of mobile data entry. You can see an excellent example in the winner of the 2003 Imagine Cup (*http://www.imaginecup.com*), a programming contest that Microsoft sponsors for college students. I helped to judge the finals at Tech-

Ed Europe, and Tu Nguyen's bilingual data entry system for waiters in his family's Vietnamese restaurant knocked my socks off. The chef, his father, spoke little English, and bilingual Vietnamese waiters are hard to find in Omaha, Nebraska. So Tu put the restaurant's menu onto a Pocket PC. Waiters would enter the customers' orders by checking controls with English labels in a dedicated Pocket PC application and send them to a server over a wireless network. The server contained a translation table that converted them into Vietnamese and sent them to a printer in the kitchen. Orders got to the chef more quickly because waiters didn't have to walk to the kitchen or queue for a single entry terminal. The wastage rate and flow disruption due to misunderstood orders plummeted, and the angry customer saying, "This isn't what I ordered," became a thing of the past. Faster order processing led to faster table turnover in the small restaurant, increasing their sales per square foot. It became possible to reliably tailor a dish to the diner's taste, adding extra broccoli or omitting the cilantro, which increased customer satisfaction, and hence return visits, and also improved reviews and word-of-mouth publicity.

They work well in dedicated, not generic, roles.

The waiters didn't use Word or Excel, or manage their calendars or contacts, or even play solitaire, at least not while their bosses were watching. But this small, simple, beautifully tailored system dramatically lowered the friction of almost every aspect of running this restaurant. It's under consideration for use in Omaha's new sports stadium, and I imagine that Tu Nguyen will have his choice of job offers on graduation, if he doesn't run with it himself. You can see the usefulness of this sort of application anywhere, from medicine to retail to car rental. It's a heck of a potential, but you need to think outside the generic PC box.

Location-based services are the second, probably much larger, category of mobile device applications.

The second major use that I see for mobile devices is for location-based services, by which I mean services tailored to the instantaneous physical location of a roving user. Adding global positioning system (GPS) location to a Pocket PC is cheap, and some even come with it standard. Once you know a user's latitude and longitude, it's easy to provide a map of his locale or directions to where he wants to go. The inconvenience of entering the small amount of text needed to identify the destination is small compared to the convenience of instant directions from anywhere to anywhere else. These directions can be to a particular location ("How do I get to 123 Maple St?") or to a service whose location you don't know ("How do I get to the nearest open gas station, or currency-exchanging bank, or hospital emergency room?"). Almost no one cares about carrying his task list with him electronically. But conversely, almost no one on planet Earth has not, within the past month, scratched his head and said, "Where the heck am I?" or "How do I get [somewhere] from here?", often both together.

Almost everyone already carries a cell phone, so software written for it would start with a large installed base.

This is where the Smartphone comes in. Microsoft Smartphone 2003 is a subset of the Pocket PC operating system that runs on intelligent cell phones. It's new to the market, and only a few phones currently (Feb. 2004) support it (two in the U.S., two in Europe, and four in Asia, according to Microsoft's website). It has a relatively large screen, as shown in Figure 5-2. As you can see, Microsoft is marketing them with the same misguided contacts–calendar–task list approach that hasn't convinced users to buy Pocket PCs. If most users find the Pocket PC screen and input restrictions too annoying to buy one, then only the tiniest hard core will put up with the tighter restrictions of the Smartphone. On the other hand, almost every adult and teenager in the developed world already owns a cell phone, and so does any person with money in the developing world. You don't have to bang your head against the wall to get them to carry the new kind of box; they already do that because they find basic telephone service to be useful on its own. If you have a killer application for it, they might buy your phone instead of someone else's. But you need to think about what else real people want their phones to do, and it's not carrying their to-do lists. Nor is it the constant jangling of extraneous nonsense like the sports scores or stock updates so beloved by marketing types, as with the new SPOT watch.[3] (Being immersed in a sea of this pushy noise is my idea of hell.)

Figure 5-2   Smartphone

Standard productivity applications are even less useful on a Smartphone than they are on a Pocket PC, but tailored applications could really rock.

Suppose, however, that your cell phone could, at the touch of a button, get its own location from onboard GPS and display a map of your current location and directions to somewhere else. Imagine the TV commercial–a woman driving alone, lost in the bad part of town, on a dark rainy night, with the gas gauge running low. Cut to a shot of the husband tucking the sweet six-year-old daughter into bed, smoothing her hair, saying, "Don't worry, darling, Mommy will be home soon," but looking out the win-

---

3 Columnist Hiawatha Bray wrote in the Boston Globe for February 2, 2004: "SPOT lacks a reason to exist in any form, at any price. Most of us can pass an hour or two without reading the latest stock quotes. The few who must have a constant flow of information also need the ability to act on that information, an ability that SPOT doesn't provide. So these news junkies don't need it either. Above all, nobody needs a watch this ugly. Nobody."

dow with worried face. Back to the car: she pulls out the Microsoft Smartphone that her loving husband paid a little extra for because she's worth it, that doesn't take much more room in her purse. One push of a button, and lo! The phone's speaker activates and a soothing voice says, "Take the next left to the highway onramp." A map appears on the phone's screen, with a bright green arrow pointing the way home, and an outside shot shows her car accelerating up the ramp past a menacing bad-guy shadow (possibly dousing it with wheel spray). Final image: car pulls into comfortable suburban driveway, little girl's voice shouts, "Mommy! I'm so glad you're home!" Close-up shot of woman's face relaxing, she sighs, "Me, too." Screen text and voiceover: "Microsoft. Where do YOU want to go today?" Did you manage to finish reading that description without yanking out your credit card to buy one? Writing software for the Smartphone has enormous potential, once you think about what people really want. I demonstrate this application in this chapter's second example, and it was surprisingly easy to write.

We'd like to use the same programming model across all compact devices.

What do we need to write software for these devices? First, even though they vary much more than desktop PCs, we would really like to program in a similar manner from one type of compact device to another. Programming a Dell desktop PC is exactly like programming a Compaq or a Sony PC. Such differences as do exist, say, video resolution, we can discover dynamically via the operating system, calling exactly the same function on one platform as on another. In the compact world, we'd like programming a Hewlett-Packard iPAQ 1945 to be as similar as possible to programming a Toshiba e405, because we'd like the same application to run on all of them. Any differences, such as the presence of an onboard camera or GPS, we want to be able to detect in the same manner from one platform to another.

We need it to be efficient on these smaller, tighter systems.

Second, these compact devices share the problem of tight resources. For example, the Samsung i600 Smartphone shown previously in Figure 5-2 has a 200-MHz processor and 32 MB of RAM. While this is tight compared to a modern-day PC, it wasn't all that long ago that a desktop with that capability would have been considered a screamer, not a boat anchor. I successfully ran Windows NT 4.0 and Visual C++ on a PC with those exact specifications as recently as 2000. (It was Word's performance that caused me to dump that box.) Since an intelligent device generally serves one user at a time, scalability doesn't figure into the equation. And unlike a PC, a mobile device generally runs only one application at a time, due to the limited screen size if nothing else. A standard Pocket PC screen is 240 pixels wide by 320 high, roughly 10 percent of the pixels available on a 1024 × 768 monitor. A Smartphone screen is 176 × 180 pixels, roughly 4 percent. We want our programming tools to produce efficient code to run on these smaller, tighter systems.

We'd like all the rapid development features of .NET to transfer to the compact device world.

We'd like the process of developing intelligent device applications to be as smooth as the other parts of the .NET environment that we've come to love. Features such as free choice of language, inheritance, and garbage collection make our lives so much easier that we need to take these with us into the mobile device world. We'd like to transfer the skill sets we already have. That, to my mind, is Microsoft's primary advantage over other smart device development platforms.

We'd like easy access to geographical databases and cell phone location services.

When we start thinking about location-based services, our smart devices will need some help. They generally don't carry enough storage space for geographical databases used for driving directions, as you'll find on DVD in car-based navigation systems. We need a way for that sort of information to sit outside of the compact device, yet be easy for our programs to access. Furthermore, the problem of finding a cell phone's instantaneous location is non-trivial. Many of them won't have onboard GPS for some time, and others will determine their locations with different blends of GPS and varying types of help from their radio networks. We'd like one common interface that will allow us to find the location of a cell phone regardless of the technology that it uses to determine that location.

Solution Architecture

Microsoft has wanted to enter the compact device market for some time.

Microsoft has wanted to make operating systems for non-PC devices for much longer than most people think, but so far they haven't earned anywhere near the market share they have on the desktop. I remember teaching the Windows SDK for a user group back in 1993, at which a Microsoft evangelist preached what they were then calling "Windows Everywhere." We snickered at it, called it "Windows for Washing Machines," and wished he'd shut up so we could get to the bar (sorry, James). But Microsoft is nothing if not persistent, and they kept on coming.

Windows XP Embedded is a PC-sized operating system for embedded devices.

Microsoft has two main products in the devices arena, Windows XP Embedded and Windows CE. The former is a componentized version of the full Windows XP operating system. It runs on PC-like devices, such as the Internet refrigerator sold by LG Electronics. It supports all Windows XP drivers. It allows vendors to pick and choose which items to include, but it's not designed to be resource constrained as for a Pocket PC. It's easy for an administrator to lock down so that even a smart user can't bring up a porn movie on an airline check-in kiosk. (I tried. No dice. Not yet, anyway.) You program it with the standard .NET Framework I've written about in other books, so I won't be discussing Windows XP Embedded any more in this book.

Windows CE runs on small, tight devices.

The other, more interesting one (to me) is Windows CE.[4] This product is a subset of the Win32 operating system designed to run on smaller, resource-constrained devices

---

[4] Microsoft hates to hear people do it, but I have never heard anyone who isn't a Microsoft employee pronounce the name of this operating system as anything other than "wince," as in grimace of pain. The users don't dislike it any more than any other software product, but how can you ignore an acronym like that when someone drops it in your lap? Whoever names operating systems at Microsoft should study Homer Simpson. In an early episode he has to choose a name for his newborn son and tries to find one that the other kids won't tease him about. He says, "Let's see: Bart, Cart, Dart, Ee-art ... Nope, can't see any problem with that!"

such as personal information managers and Smartphones. It first shipped in 1996 on the launch platform of a Cassiopeia PDA, if memory serves. As always with a first release of anything, the silence was deafening and users stayed away in droves. It's gone through several revisions and is now known as Windows CE .NET, even though it's still a straight function-based C-language API that doesn't have anything to do with the .NET Framework. Windows CE also comes in a version called Windows Mobile 2003, which is a smaller subset for the Pocket PC platform, and Smartphone 2003, a still smaller subset for smart cell phones.

The Microsoft .NET Compact Framework runs on top of Windows CE.

Until now, developers have programmed Windows CE with a tool called eMbedded (why always this annoying capitalization?) Visual C++ and eMbedded Visual Basic. To make it easier, Microsoft developed the .NET Compact Framework. This essentially is a slimmed-down version of the .NET Framework that runs on top of Windows CE, just as the full .NET Framework runs on top of the full Win32 operating system. The .NET Compact Framework brings the benefits of language independence, garbage collection, JIT compilation, and so on to the embedded world. The Compact Framework also comes in versions for the Pocket PC and Smartphone. It allows developers to develop faster with fewer bugs. It often ships in the device's ROM, so as to save application space.

The performance hit of the Compact Framework is more than made up by the faster development time and fewer bugs.

As I've said many times in previous books about a new feature, "Oh yeah? What does it cost?" Obviously a garbage collector consumes more of the compact device's precious memory and processor cycles than would a simple heap allocator. But the capacity of these devices has grown to the point where this is now a profitable tradeoff. Mobile applications are now so sophisticated that they're limited more by the ability of developers to write bug-free code and the input and output constraints of the platform than by sheer processor power and memory size. Microsoft has worked very hard to make the Compact Framework as efficient as it can be. At a certain point, it takes money to make money. You need the advanced capabilities to write applications that stand out, and don't crash, at least not as often.

The obvious question is: What parts of the .NET Framework does the Compact Framework support? The raw numbers look approximately like this:

	Classes	Methods
Full .NET Framework	18,700	80,000
Compact Framework	4700	13,000

Many classes have been removed from the Compact Framework.

You can see quickly from Figure 5-3 which groups of classes the Compact Framework contains and has had removed. All the server-side pieces have been removed, such as System.Web.UI controls. So have such items as the System.Drawing.Imaging namespace, whose advanced drawing capabilities have limited utility on a compact device screen. Many of the lowest-level programming capabilities have been completely or partially removed. For example, in the System.Runtime namespace, Remoting has been completely removed, InteropServices supports P/Invoke for calling native API functions directly but not COM, but most of Reflection is still there. The idea is to leave the classes that are useful to small, light, client-side applications. While the "Whidbey" release is expected to add many more classes and methods, it's too early to say with any certainty which ones they will or won't be. It's also too early to say what mechanism, if any, will be available for removing the ones you don't care about to save space.

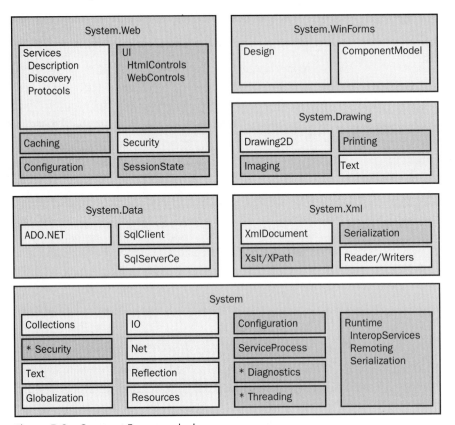

Figure 5-3   Compact Framework classes.

The remaining classes have been slimmed down.

The classes that do remain have been slimmed down as much as possible. For example, to save space and cycles, the Compact Framework garbage collector does not support different generations of objects, as the full .NET Framework garbage collector does. The methods that deal with generations, such as GetGeneration, have been removed from the Compact Framework System.GC class. A method that still exists might have some of its overloads removed. For example, System.GC.Collect exists in both full and compact Frameworks, but the overload that allows you to specify a particular generation to collect doesn't exist in the Compact Framework because generations don't.

The online documentation supports a filter that displays only Compact Framework classes.

You can see the classes available by selecting the .NET Compact Framework filter in the online documentation, as shown in Figure 5-4. This displays all classes that have any methods available in the Compact Framework. The individual topic entries, such as the garbage collector shown, don't change. Each method or property that is supported by the Compact Framework contains a notation to that effect. In the figure, you can see that GetGeneration doesn't, but the rest do.

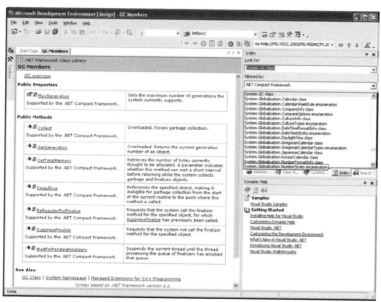

Figure 5-4   Visual Studio documentation displaying Compact Framework classes and methods.

Visual Studio supports .NET Compact Framework projects with its usual look and feel.

Microsoft Visual Studio makes Compact Framework projects look and feel very much like desktop projects. This is similar to the way it makes Web projects look and feel like desktop projects. As is also the case with Web projects, sometimes this look and feel is truthful and sometimes it isn't. As always, you need to understand what you're really doing in a compact device application (and in a Web application, and in a desktop application, too). Since a compact device doesn't have room for a real debugger, Visual Studio contains software emulators that do. You use these for most testing and debugging of your applications. This support is much easier to demonstrate than it is to describe. So let's go have a look.

Microsoft provides geographical data through the MapPoint Web Service.

Microsoft provides the MapPoint Web Service (*http://www.mappoint.net*) to allow mobile device programs to access geographical data over the wireless Internet. It's a standard SOAP-based Web service, which your client applications consume in the same manner as any other. MapPoint can generate a map for a specified latitude and longitude, find the latitude and longitude of a specified street address, and give driving directions from one latitude and longitude point to another. It even has a database containing the location of various business establishments, which you can search by type and according to distance from a specified latitude and longitude point. Once you find the business you want, you can feed its location to the map and directions algorithms. The last sample program in this chapter demonstrates the MapPoint Web Service used on a Smartphone.

Microsoft is just now rolling out an easy cell phone locator service.

Microsoft is in the process of adding cell phone location capabilities to MapPoint via its MapPoint Location Server. It's officially scheduled to go live just as this book goes to press (late March 2004), so I can't demonstrate it or say too much about it now. It should be commercially available by the time you read this. Basically, it is a SOAP-based Web service that allows you to make a call saying, "Here's the cell phone I want to track, and here's the credential you need to look me up to see if I'm authorized to know that phone's location. Now give me the phone's latitude and longitude." The service abstracts away the differences from one provider to another, and from one location technology to another, whether the phone is using full onboard precision GPS, or triangulating off the cell phone towers with no GPS at all, or some combination of the two. Watch for an article in *MSDN* magazine in summer of 2004 and on this book's website for more information. My MLS-enrolled Smartphone is on its way to me as I write these words. It was shipped with its power turned on, so I can track its instantaneous location online. It's now on Old Right Road in Ipswich, MA—about 6 miles (10 km) away from me and heading in my direction. Oops, he's turned onto Route 133; he's only about 4 miles out. It's probably time to get out of my pajamas so I can sign for it.

Simplest Example

A simple Compact Framework example starts here.

As I do with all my chapters, I created the simplest Compact Framework project I could imagine so I could describe the elements without mental noise from the business logic. This application displays the time on a Pocket PC, with or without the seconds digits, as shown in Figure 5-5. You can download it from this book's website and work along with me.

Figure 5-5   Pocket PC emulator showing the simplest example program.

It's a Windows Forms application for the Pocket PC 2003.

To make this project accessible to more users, I wrote it using Visual Studio 2003 instead of the Whidbey Alpha PDC version. I had to download the Pocket PC 2003 add-on SDK, which doesn't come with Visual Studio 2003. I created a project, selecting Smart Device Application, as shown in Figure 5-6. Visual Studio then displayed the dialog box shown in Figure 5-7 that asked me which system I wanted to target; I explained the choices in the "Solution Architecture" section. I chose Pocket PC and Windows Application.

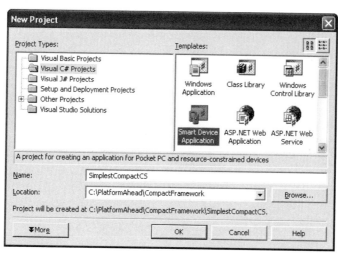

Figure 5-6   Dialog box for selecting the Smart Device project.

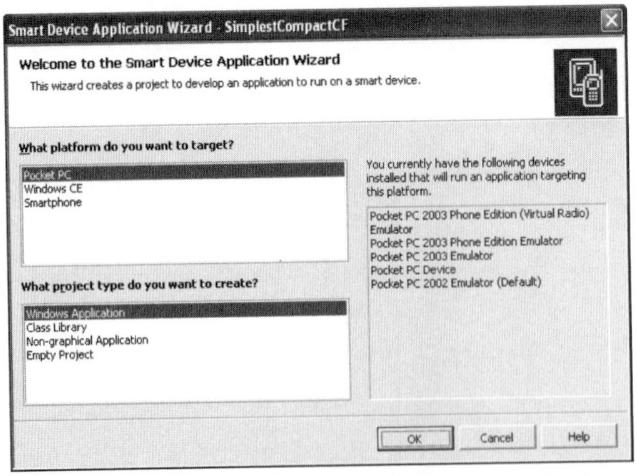

Figure 5-7   Dialog box for selecting the Smart Device project target platform.

The wizard generates a form and references.

The wizard generated the project that you see in Figure 5-8. The form has a total area of 246 pixels wide by 302 pixels high, which produces a client area of exactly the right size for a 240 × 320 pixel Pocket PC. The excess width pixels account for the fact that the PPC screen doesn't have borders, although the designer does. And the missing height pixels account for the area consumed by title and status bars. The wizard has also generated project references that seem familiar, such as MSCorLib and System. If you check the path of these DLLs, you'll see that they live in the CompactFrameworkSDK subfolder, instead of the standard reference folder.

Most of the classes feel similar, but a few differences exist.

Now that I had a form, I dragged controls onto it from the Visual Studio toolbox, as I'm used to doing. I chose a button, a check box, and a label. Double-clicking the button added a handler function to my form class, again in the familiar manner. When I looked at the code for my form class, I saw that it derived from the familiar system base class System.Windows.Forms.Form. At least superficially, it looks like what I'm used to from desktop forms applications. But if you look at it a little more deeply, you'll see some changes for the Compact Framework. As I showed in the previous section, the Compact Framework contains fewer than half the classes and a quarter of the methods of the full .NET Framework. When I looked at the IntelliSense list of the form's methods and properties, I saw that some of the familiar framework properties were present while others were not. For example, I saw that the BackColor property is supported in the Compact Framework, which makes sense because it has a background color just like a standard form. But the HelpButton property doesn't exist in the Compact Framework because its applications generally don't have enough room to carry the online help files that this button would bring up–it makes sense to save space by omitting it.

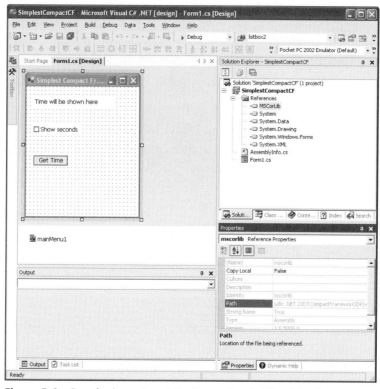

Figure 5-8   Developing a Smart Device project in Visual Studio.

The usual building and debugging commands work similarly on a Compact Framework application.

I wrote the code you see in Listing 5-1, which gets the time and displays it in the label control. You can see that it's exactly the same as for a desktop application. I next wanted to build and debug it. Start from the Visual Studio menu, which launched the Pocket PC 2003 emulator and downloaded the program to it, as shown previously in Figure 5-5. I can run my program, set breakpoints, and examine data, just as for a standard Windows Forms application.

Listing 5-1   Simplest .NET Compact Framework example.

```
// This function gets called when the user clicks
// the GetTime button. Note that this code looks
// and feels the same as for a desktop application.

private void button1_Click(object sender, System.EventArgs e)
{
    // If the user has checked the Show Seconds box,
    // then display the time with the seconds digits.

    if (checkBox1.Checked == true)
    {
        label1.Text = DateTime.Now.ToLongTimeString() ;
    }

    // Otheriwse, display the time without the
    // seconds digits.

    else
    {
        label1.Text = DateTime.Now.ToShortTimeString() ;
    }
}
```

Visual Studio can generate a .CAB file for installing the application on the Pocket PC. Finally, I wanted to deploy this program to an actual Pocket PC and run it there. Again, this was quite easy with the Visual Studio development environment. I right-clicked the project and selected Build Cab File. This generated the directory shown in Figure 5-9. Each of the .CAB folders is the installation for a specific processor type used by smart devices. In my case, the HP iPAQ 5500 contains an ARM processor. I placed the .CAB file into a folder I had shared on the network and ran it from my Pocket PC browser. That installed the program, so now I can run this fantastically useful application on my Pocket PC any time I can tear myself away from Solitaire.

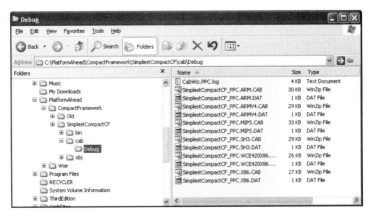

Figure 5-9   .CAB files for different Pocket PC platforms.

The JIT compiler on the target device produces the native code.

Despite the fact that there is a separate installation for each type of processor, the .NET assembly and the IL it contains remain unchanged. I can demonstrate this by opening the new Compact Framework assembly in the intermediate language disassembler tool, ILDASM, as shown in Figure 5-10. The JIT compiler on each device converts it into that device's processor's native code.

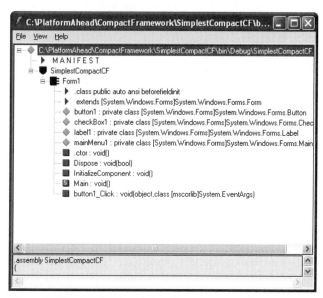

Figure 5-10   ILDASM tool showing contents of Compact Framework assembly.

That's a very simple user interface application running on a compact device. Expanding that to a dedicated input program of the type I described in the opening section is tedious but not difficult. I find the thought of location-based services much more exciting, so let's go look at them.

Complex Example: Location-Based Services Using the Smartphone

Almost every adult and teenager in the developed world carries a cell phone, so a killer app for them would make a lot of money.

Having explored a Pocket PC, I next wanted to write an application for a Smartphone. As I stated previously, not many people currently carry a Pocket PC, but everyone in the world with enough money for us to care about separating him from it carries a phone. If we can write a killer app for it, they might buy our phones next time they need one.

I think that location maps and directions are that killer application.

That killer app, it seems to me, would be fast, easy maps and directions based on a user's current location. Every family in the world would want it for car safety, as opposed to the tiny fraction of pathetic geeks that would go to the trouble of putting their grocery lists on their cell phones. I decided to demonstrate the simplest location-based service I could find.

The sample program is a rich client for Microsoft's Map-Point Web Service.

The sample program is a rich client for Microsoft's MapPoint Web Service, which I've previously described. The sample program provides the interface for getting input from the user, making requests to MapPoint, and displaying the results. Because most of the brains are on the Web Service side, I'm astounded at how much useful functionality I was able to concoct with just a few lines of code.

MapPoint is a commercial service. Please don't abuse this book's sample account.

> **Warning**   MapPoint is a commercial service for which Microsoft charges access fees. Making calls to MapPoint requires an account for billing and a user ID and password to authorize access to the account. I've obtained a demonstration account for the purpose of this book, and the sample code contains the user ID and password for this account. The MapPoint team warns that: "If this shared account is discovered to be abused (someone takes it and begins to do high-volume commercial stuff, for instance), we will terminate the account. We've never had to do this, because the vast majority of developers are more honest than people give them credit for." Please don't make a liar out of them, or a bigger fool out of me. If you're going to do anything other than run my sample a few times to see how it works, please get your own free trial account at *http://www.microsoft.com/mappoint/webservice/default.mspx*.

The Smartphone user interface is different because of hardware constraints.

I downloaded and installed the Smartphone 2003 SDK from the Microsoft website. The SDK contains the emulators and documentation that Visual Studio needed to recognize the target platform. I generated a Compact Framework project in Visual Studio and chose Smartphone 2003 from the target platform dialog box. The wizard generated a form for me whose client area is 176 pixels wide by 180 pixels high, which is the size of the screen's available client area, minus the title bar and the menu buttons that I'll describe next. You can see the Visual Studio environment displaying this form in Figure 5-11. The Smartphone requires a different user interface than the Pocket PC, because it lacks a touch screen and stylus for entering data and commands. Instead, the user enters commands via the two buttons that you see in the figure just below the screen. They're called softkeys even though they are quite hard, because their actions change with the menu item labels shown above them by the application. The left-hand softkey is generally used for one-touch activation of the most important command. For example, in Solitaire, it's draw from the pile. The right-hand one generally provides access to a list of context menu items, as does the right-click on the desktop. The user can navigate with the arrow keys and the home and back buttons. Alphabetic and numeric data is entered on the numeric keys, using repeated keystrokes for letters.

> Note   At the time of this writing, none of the Smartphone units commercially available in the United States run the Smartphone 2003 operating system, and thus support the Compact Framework natively. The two available phones I spoke of earlier run Smartphone 2002, which doesn't. The pre-production phones that run the 2003 operating system are on their way to developers as I write these words (mine is just down the block now, the locator service tells me) and will be featured prominently at Microsoft's Mobile Device Conference the last week of March 2004. I would expect them to arrive on the commercial market by summer of 2004 and to make hot presents for Christmas that year.

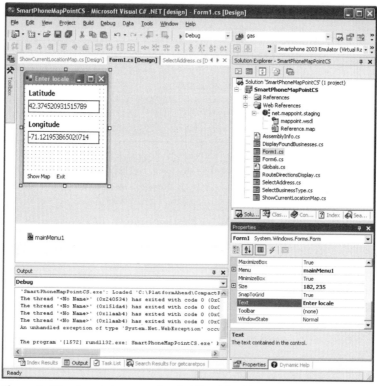

Figure 5-11   Smartphone project in Visual Studio.

Smartphones will soon support automatic location, but in this example you enter latitude and longitude with a form.

This program starts by displaying a form for entering the user's latitude and longitude. This is a hack for the purpose of this example. The emulator and, for that matter, the phone don't currently come equipped with any sort of location service. But United States emergency service regulations will require 95 percent of phones to be so equipped by 2005, so it's coming soon. In fact, Microsoft's MapPoint Locator Service is scheduled to go live just after this book's press deadline. This service will provide a convenient SOAP interface that will abstract away the differences between various carriers' and phones' location technologies and allow a programmer to fetch a phone user's location with a single Web Service call. Watch this book's website for information on upcoming articles on it. For the sample program, I placed text boxes on the screen for latitude and longitude, and labels for each. The phone already has an input method editor for entering text and numbers into the text boxes, so you don't have to get involved with that. The user moves from one text box to the next by using the arrow keys. The default location is Harvard Square in Cambridge, which those of us who work there modestly admit is the Hub of the Universe. Clicking the Show Map softkey sends you to the next page, which is where a production app would start.

I next generated a proxy for accessing the MapPoint Web Service.

To fetch maps, locations, and directions, my program needs to access the MapPoint service, so the next thing I did was to set up access to it. I downloaded the MapPoint SDK from the Microsoft website. It contains documentation and samples, but no DLLs or other code. Since MapPoint is a Web Service, you access it by means of a client-side proxy. I generated this proxy, as for any other Web Service, by right-clicking the project folder and selecting Add Web Reference from the context menu. I gave the proxy generator the address, specified in the SDK, for the service's WSDL file, and it generated the proxy. You can see the Web reference if you look carefully at Figure 5-11. Since I needed to make Web Service calls from various points in my program, I added a class called "Globals" that contains methods for accessing the MapPoint service. That's also where I store the user ID and password for sending with the MapPoint requests, and other data items that are potentially useful at different parts of the application, such as the latitude and longitude of the phone itself.

I pass the latitude, longitude, and rendering options to MapPoint, and it gives me back a picture containing a map.

The second form, called ShowCurrentLocationMap, uses MapPoint's Render service to render a map of the area around the phone's current location. Listing 5-2 shows my method Globals.GetMap( ), which does the actual Web Service call. Within it, I allocate and set the parameters required by MapPoint. The call requires an object of class MapSpec. This contains an object of class MapView, which tells the service which portion of the world to map. In this case, I specify a center point (the latitude and longitude of the phone) and a scaling factor. There are several other ways to specify the extent of the map, as we'll see in later cases. I also specify a MapOptions object, which describes how I want the map to be rendered. In this case, I specify the size of the bitmap that I want in return, along with zooming and panning factors I'll discuss later. Finally, I specify an array of PushPins objects, which specifies the markers I want added to the map. In this case I put in only one, indicating the user's current location on the map. On a large-scale map they can look like little push pins, but at this small scale it's just a little circle.

Listing 5-2   Web Service call fetching map from MapPoint service.

```
public static Bitmap GetMap (LatLong centerPoint, double ZoomFactor,
double PanHorizontal, double PanVertical)
{

    // Set up the map specification object
    MapSpecification mapSpec = new MapSpecification ();

    // Set the data source name in the map specification
    mapSpec.DataSourceName = "MapPoint.NA";

    // Create an array of MapView objects, which
    // contains one member, of class ViewByScale
    ViewByScale[] views = new ViewByScale[1];
    views [0] = new ViewByScale ( ) ;
    mapSpec.Views = views ;

    // Set the center point of the view to the
    // location of the phone

    views[0].CenterPoint = centerPoint   ;
    views[0].MapScale = scale ;

    //Set the map options

    mapSpec.Options = new MapOptions ();

    mapSpec.Options.Format = new ImageFormat ();
    mapSpec.Options.Format.Height = 296;
    mapSpec.Options.Format.Width = 292;
    mapSpec.Options.Zoom = ZoomFactor;
    mapSpec.Options.PanHorizontal = PanHorizontal;
    mapSpec.Options.PanVertical = PanVertical;
    mapSpec.Options.Style = MapStyle.Phone ;

    // Create the pushpin array and put it in the map spec
    // This one places the user at the center

    mapSpec.Pushpins = new Pushpin[1];
    mapSpec.Pushpins[0] = new Pushpin ();
    mapSpec.Pushpins[0].PinID = "0";
    mapSpec.Pushpins[0].Label = "You";
    mapSpec.Pushpins[0].IconName = "0";
    mapSpec.Pushpins[0].IconDataSource = "MapPoint.Icons";
    mapSpec.Pushpins[0].LatLong = views [0].CenterPoint;
    mapSpec.Pushpins[0].LabelNearbyRoads = true;

    // Make the call to get the map.

    MapImage[] myMapImages ;
    try
    {
        // Get the rendered map

        RenderServiceSoap prx = new RenderServiceSoap ( ) ;
        prx.Credentials = new NetworkCredential (userID, password) ;
        prx.PreAuthenticate = true ;
```

```
        myMapImages = prx.GetMap (mapSpec) ;

        // Convert it into a bitmap

        Bitmap b = new Bitmap (new System.IO.MemoryStream
                (myMapImages[0].MimeData.Bits));

        return b ;
    }

    catch (Exception x)
    {
        <handle exception >
    {

    return null ;
}
```

When the map comes back, I display it in a picture box.

When the MapPoint request is complete, I convert the bits into an actual Bitmap object and display the bitmap in the PictureBox control that the form contains for this purpose. That's all I have to do to display a user's location. Figure 5-12 shows the Smartphone displaying a user location map obtained from MapPoint.

Figure 5-12   Your location displayed on the Smartphone.

Adding scrolling by hooking the KeyDown event is an easy task.

I wanted to enhance my locating application with a few more features, so I added scrolling, zooming, and panning. None of them was at all difficult. The screen client area is only 176 × 180 pixels, so it's likely that the user will need to scroll it up or down a little to see all the geographical area that she cares about. I could make a separate Web request for each scroll, but the data transmission overhead of a Web Service call is somewhat high, plus MapPoint charges by the hit (currently about 1.5–3 cents US, with discounts for large quantities). So I request a 296 × 300 pixel image with each map rendering call and display only the center 176 × 180 pixels of it. That leaves 60 pixels of image available for scrolling on each edge of the screen. To accept scrolling commands from the user, I added a handler for the form's "KeyDown," using the code shown in Listing 5-3. This event gets fired when the user presses any key. You generally ignore it for text input, allowing text boxes to handle that functionality, but it's useful for the navigation keys. The KeyEventArgs parameter contains a property called Key-Code, specifying which key the user has clicked. The Left and Right keys move the picture horizontally and the Up and Down keys vertically. All I do to move the image is change the picture box's location relative to the form. The scroll bar controls on the side of the window don't actually cause the screen to move, as they do in desktop applications. Rather, they indicate the current location of the scroll, telling the user how far he can go in either direction. I set their positions with function calls, as you can see.

Listing 5-3   Keystroke event handler performing scrolling and panning map.

```
private void Form2_KeyDown (object sender, System.Windows.Forms.KeyEventArgs e)
{
    // Check for the arrow keys. Scroll if found.

    switch (e.KeyCode)
    {
        case Keys.Left:

            // If we haven't hit the limit of the map, then change the
            // origin of the pixture box to show the hidden pixels.

            if (hScrollBar2.Value > 0)
            {
                hScrollBar2.Value--;
                pictureBox1.Left = -(20 * hScrollBar2.Value);
            }
            // We've hit the left-hand edge, so we need to pan the map.
            // Subtract 50 % from the pan factor

            else
            {
                PanHorizontal -= 0.5;
                MyOwnCoughUpMap ();
            }

            break;

            <other key cases>
    }
}
```

MapPoint easily supports panning when the user reaches the scrolling boundary.

When the user scrolls to the edge of the available map and tries to continue, she's asking to leave the area for which I currently have a display map. She can continue if I pan the map by making another MapPoint call to obtain a map of the adjacent area. MapPoint's Render service supports this easily, by accepting the PanHorizontal and PanVertical parameters in the MapOptions object. These specify the percentages by which the returned map should be offset from the specified center point. All I do to pan my map is to increment (east or north) or decrement (west or south) the panning factor and re-request the map. It doesn't get much easier than that.

Adding zooming was likewise easy.

Having used the arrow keys for scrolling, I implemented zooming with menu item commands. You add menu items to the Smartphone form using the Visual Studio menu editor, in a manner similar to a desktop application. You add handler functions to the form by double-clicking the menu item. The only difficulty I had was that the editor allowed me to add menu items to the left-hand softkey menu, but the operating system threw an exception when I tried to run the form containing that menu, thus enforcing the user interface convention of the left-hand softkey invoking a single item. In the menu item handler functions, I simply multiply or divide a zooming factor that I maintain for this purpose and re-request the map.

These were so easy that I decided to add directions to the Smartphone sample.

I'd gotten all of this done quickly and I was really on a roll, so I wanted to see how many features I could add before the press deadline. I wondered how hard it would be to get directions, and the answer is "not at all." Since the most common request for directions is, "How do I get home from here?", I added a menu item to handle that specific case. For this example, I recorded the phone's home latitude and longitude in my Globals object. A production app would probably record the user's current location in nonvolatile memory when she pushed a button telling it to remember. It could probably record any reasonable number of waypoints and destinations (your office, tonight's hotel) in this manner.

MapPoint will return a set of driving directions for an array of longitude and latitude points.

MapPoint provides directions through its Route service. You pass this method RouteService.CalculateSimpleRoute, specifying an array of latitude and longitude points through which you want to travel. In this example, they're the phone's current location and the hard-wired location of wherever home is. The service returns an object of class Route, containing human-readable directions and information for rendering a map of the route. You can see the code for this in Listing 5-4.

Listing 5-4   Call to MapPoint's Route service for directions.

```
public static Route GetRoute (LatLong from, LatLong to)
{
    // Create an array of 2 LatLong objects

    LatLong[] lls = new LatLong[2];

    // Set their values to those passed by the caller
```

```
lls[0] = from  ;
lls[1] = to  ;

// Calculate and return route

RouteServiceSoap prx = new RouteServiceSoap ( ) ;
prx.Credentials = new NetworkCredential(userID, password) ;
prx.PreAuthenticate = true ;

return prx.CalculateSimpleRoute (lls, "MapPoint.NA",
     SegmentPreference.Shortest);

}
```

A Route contains a list of directions for display, and information for easily rendering a map.

Once I have the route, I need to display it to the user, as shown on the left in Figure 5-13. The property Route.Itinerary.Segments contains an array of strings, one for each segment of the route. I wrote a form class that displays these arrays on a scrollable List-View on the phone screen. You can see this listing in the sample code. You might also like to display a map of the route. You can easily do this by passing the Route object in the MapSpec object in a call to RenderService.GetMap( ), as shown in the sample code and the screen on the right in Figure 5-13.

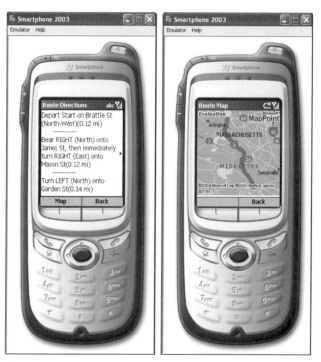

Figure 5-13   Displaying a route and viewing a map on a Smartphone.

MapPoint's Find service returns the latitude and longitude of a specified street address.

All the features I've just shown are handy if we have latitude and longitude points, but most people and businesses don't publish, or usually even know, theirs.[5] Fortunately, MapPoint provides us with services that can give us the latitude and longitude for a specified street address. You do that with the backwards-named method FindService.FindAddress( ). I added a menu item saying "Directions to Address." When you select it, you'll see a form for entering the desired address, which I've filled with preselected values. When you select the Show Directions menu item on it, I call this method, as you'll see in Listing 5-5. This returns a latitude and longitude, which I then pass to the route display logic I just wrote about. It may, however, return several choices, or none, and a production app will have to provide logic for sorting it out.

Listing 5-5 Call to MapPoint service requesting latitude and longitude of a street address.

```
public static LatLong FindAddress (string StreetAddr, string city,
    string state)
{

    // Get lat and long for specified street address
    // Create and populate Address object for FindAddress() operation.

    Address myAddress = new Address ();
    myAddress.AddressLine = StreetAddr ;
    myAddress.PrimaryCity  = city ;
    myAddress.Subdivision  = state ;

    // Set up address specification object
    FindAddressSpecification findAddressSpec =
            new FindAddressSpecification ();

    findAddressSpec.InputAddress = myAddress;
    findAddressSpec.DataSourceName = "MapPoint.NA";

    FindServiceSoap fss = new FindServiceSoap ( ) ;
    fss.Credentials = new NetworkCredential (userID, password) ;
    fss.PreAuthenticate = true ;

    // make call, get results
    FindResults myFindResults = fss.FindAddress (findAddressSpec);

    return myFindResults.Results[0].FoundLocation.LatLong ;

}
```

---

5 A notable exception is the Delorme mapping company, whose website proudly proclaims that you will find them at Latitude 43°48.491' North, Longitude 70°09.844' West. Go look them up on the Smartphone sample. You'll have to convert the latitude and longitude to decimal.

MapPoint can also find instances of a specified type of business near a specified point.

Finally, suppose we don't know the street address of our destination, or even its name. MapPoint provides access to a number of business locator databases. In this example, I show the user a form offering a choice of gas stations, ATMs, or brew pubs, establishments offering all the types of fuel a guy could need. When the user makes his selection, I call the FindService's FindNearby method, which provides a list of those types of establishments. The code is shown in Listing 5-6 and the results in Figure 5-14. The sample shows a list of them, but the results could easily be placed on a map instead. Once the user selects one, I fetch its latitude and longitude with the Find service, get directions with the Route service, and display them to the user with the logic I've previously discussed.

Figure 5-14   Locating a business address

Listing 5-6   Call to MapPoint requesting location of nearby businesses.

```
public static FindResults FindNearbyBusiness (string businessCode)
{
    // Create new Find Nearby Specification

    FindNearbySpecification fns = new FindNearbySpecification ();

    // Select Data source

    fns.DataSourceName = "NavTech.NA";
```

```
    // Set nearby distance

    fns.Distance = 10;

    // Set latitude and longitude to search around

    fns.LatLong = PhoneLatLong;

    // Set the filter for the type of establishment chosen by user

    fns.Filter = new FindFilter ();
    fns.Filter.EntityTypeName = businessCode ;

    // Make the call

    FindServiceSoap fss = new FindServiceSoap ( ) ;
    fss.Credentials = new NetworkCredential (userID, password) ;
    fss.PreAuthenticate = true ;

    return fss.FindNearby (fns);
}
```

Obviously a production application will have better error handling, a smoother user interface, and a richer feature set than this simple prototype. For example, I'd probably take the scrolling/zooming/panning map display capability and use it on the directions map display and the business type map display. But I'm astounded at what I managed to get to totter to its feet and say hello in return for very little effort. This is about the richest prototype I've ever done in my life, and it wasn't very hard. So never mind those dumb to-do lists, or even the solitaire game. The beauty of mobile devices is that they know where you are. There's more money here than I can count. And I can count a lot.

Chapter 6
Contradiction

There's a land where the mountains are nameless,
  And the rivers all run God knows where;
There are lives that are erring and aimless,
  And deaths that just hang by a hair;
There are hardships that nobody reckons;
  There are valleys unpeopled and still;
There's a land – oh, it beckons and beckons,
  And I want to go back – and I will.

They're making my money diminish;
  I'm sick of the taste of champagne.
Thank God! when I'm skinned to a finish
  I'll pike to the Yukon again.
I'll fight – and you bet it's no sham-fight;
  It's hell! – but I've been there before;
And it's better than this by a damnsite –
  So me for the Yukon once more.

— *Robert W. Service, "The Spell of the Yukon," stanzas 6 and 7*

My older daughter is now almost four and loves Winnie the Pooh—the real Pooh, by A. A. Milne, with drawings by Ernest H. Shepard; none of this Disney nonsense. She asks me questions like, "Daddy, why is Eeyore always so gloomy? Is it so Pooh and Piglet can cheer him up?"

My daughter loves Winnie the Pooh.

And so, when it comes time to say goodbye at the end of this book, I find it only natural to defer to Milne. "When we asked Pooh," he writes in *The House at Pooh Corner*, "what the opposite of an Introduction was, he said 'The what of a what?' which didn't help us as much as we had hoped, but luckily Owl kept his head and told us that the opposite of an Introduction, my dear Pooh, was a Contradiction; and, as he is very good at long words, I am sure that's what it is." And if he's sure, then so am I, and that's what I'll call it.

So I'll call this section a "contradiction," because that's what A. A. Milne does.

A few spring peeper frogs are just now tuning up here in New England, getting ready for the chorus that will signal the coming of spring. They don't care about versioning or throughput scalability. They sing because they sing. We're more like them than we think, my fellow geeks. We're smart enough to do anything we want and dumb enough that we choose this line of work. We program because we program. The

We program because we program.

Yukon grabbed us long ago and won't let us go. And in our heart of hearts, we don't want it to.

Peace be unto you and yours.

So until we meet again, by book or electronic newsletter (*http://www.rollthunder.com*) or in person, I'll wish peace to you and yours, and hope you'll wish the same to me and, more importantly, mine. I'll give Robert Service the last word and let him take us on out with his final stanza:

> *There's gold, and it's haunting and haunting;*
>   *It's luring me on as of old;*
> *Yet it isn't the gold that I'm wanting*
>   *So much as just finding the gold.*
> *It's the great, big, broad land 'way up yonder,*
>   *It's the forests where silence has lease;*
> *It's the beauty that thrills me with wonder,*
>   *It's the stillness that fills me with peace.*

Appendix A
SQL Server 2005

This appendix contains a chapter from a book that is not yet published. The book is *Introducing Microsoft SQL Server 2005 for Developers* by Peter DeBetta (Microsoft Press, 2005). This title is for both SQL Server and .NET developers who want to migrate to SQL Server 2005 (code name Yukon). Note that this product is still in development and, therefore, you can expect there will be changes in the finished product.

Chapter 5 User-Defined Data Types

The integration of the common language runtime (CLR) into Microsoft SQL Server 2005 gives developers much more flexibility than ever before possible. Yet all the great features I've described in the preceding chapters—from the SQL Workbench and T-SQL enhancements to XML capabilities and integration with the .NET Framework—are not in the same league as being able to create types in managed code. Managed types, or user-defined data types (UDTs), are not strictly for the database developer—they are also vital to the database architect. The individuals in these two roles will need to work together to get the most out of this new design implementation. The architect will best understand where and when to use managed types, and the programmer will best know how to implement them.

User-defined data types, usually called just user-defined types (UDTs), are by far the most complex of all the database object types you can implement with the CLR. UDTs are not simple methods or types that have predefined methods and attributes, but rather a very flexible way of extending the type system in SQL Server 2005.

When I started working with UDTs, I was concerned about how well they would perform, especially in larger databases. My fears were quickly alleviated—a well-designed UDT will, under most conditions, perform as quickly as other native SQL Server data types. The trick, of course, is to write efficient code, use the attributes appropriately, and use the correct serialization formats when implementing a UDT in .NET. As I explain the various requirements for a .NET type to be used as a UDT in SQL Server, I'll point out various features that you should pay attention to when designing your own types.

Attributes in UDTs

In Chapter 4, I promised a more detailed discussion regarding the *Format* property. Like user-defined attributes (UDAs), UDTs also require a *Serializable* attribute. This attribute allows the UDA or UDT to be serialized—but just how does it work? This is where the *Format* property comes into play. While UDAs use the *SqlUserDefinedAggregate* attribute, UDTs use the *SqlUserDefinedType* attribute; both attributes have a *Format* property. This property determines the serialization format of the type, of which there are three types: *SerializedDataWithMetadata*, *Native*, and *UserDefined*.

Format Property of the *SqlUserDefinedType* Attribute

The *Format* property is the only required property of this attribute. As I just mentioned, it has three possible values:

Format.SerializedDataWithMetadata This is simply .NET serialization. It is the most flexible of the serialization formats because all serialization is handled automatically for many different data types, including strings and reference types. Alas, this flexibility also causes it to be the slowest of the three, executing at an order of magnitude slower than the *Native* format.

Format.Native The fastest of the serialization formats, *Format.Native* uses native SQL Server binary serialization. With the speed, however, comes a lack of flexibility. This format can be used only if the public properties of the class are fixed-length, value-type data types. Mind you, there are a good number of these types, including numeric, date, and time data types, but types such as strings are not a part of this select group. If using this format, the *MaxByteSize* property cannot be specified.

Format.UserDefined And the winner is . . . *UserDefined*. This format has the flexibility of the *SerializedWithMetadata* format but without the negative performance considerations. It even has the potential to perform as well as the *Native* type. The only downside of this format is that you have to implement the serialization yourself. The class or struct must implement the *IBinarySerialize* interface and its *Write* and *Read* methods. It is the implementation of these two methods that determines how well this format performs. Also note that this property requires the *MaxByteSize* property to be specified.

> **Important** For several reasons beyond the scope of this text, it is currently unclear whether the *SerializedDataWithMetadata* format will be supported in future releases of SQL Server 2005. Because of this, Microsoft recommends avoiding the use of the *SerializedWithMetadata* serialization format. Instead, they recommend that the *Native* format be used whenever possible, and *UserDefined* when *Native* is not possible.

Optional Properties of *SqlUserDefinedType*

In addition to the properties I have already discussed, three optional properties are also available in *SqlUserDefinedType*:

MaxByteSize   This property determines the maximum size of the instance of this type. This property can't be set when you're using the *Native* serialization format, and it must be set when you're using *UserDefined*.

IsFixedLength   This property is false by default and indicates whether or not the total byte length of the type is fixed. This helps SQL Server use the type more efficiently.

IsByteOrdered   This property, false by default, is significant only when you're using *Native* or *UserDefined* serialization formats. It determines whether or not the binary representation of the type is ordered, which affects certain order-related characteristics of the UDT, such as indexing, comparison, and other ordering abilities.

Nullability in UDTs

As I mentioned in Chapter 4, all of the managed *SqlTypes* implement the *INullable* interface. The truth of the matter is that *SqlTypes* must implement this interface and must be null aware. Now because a UDT is also a managed *SqlType*, it must implement *INullable* and must also be null aware. Let's address the former point first.

INullable has a single public property defined—named *IsNull*—that is of type *Boolean*. Because a UDT must implement the *INullable* interface, it also must implement a public *IsNull* property that is of type *Boolean*. This sets *SqlTypes* apart from other system value types in .NET because it allows for *SqlTypes* to "legally contain the value null." This method is easy to implement, returning a local *Boolean* value that indicates the null state of the instance.

```
public Boolean IsNull
{
    get { return (is_Null); }
}
```

As another part of this compliance, UDTs are required to expose a public static method named *Null* with a return type of the UDT itself. Although a UDT can be created in an assembly that doesn't comply with these requirements, the assembly will still compile and can even be registered in SQL Server 2005 without raising any exceptions. However, any attempt to register the UDT itself will throw an exception.

```
public static Point Null
{
    get    {
        Point pt = new Point();
        pt.is_Null = true;
        return (pt);
    }
}
```

Conversion

In addition to being null capable, UDTs must be able to convert to and from a string value. To do this, a UDT must have another static method, named *Parse*, which has a return type of the UDT itself. This static *Parse* method must have a single parameter of type *SqlString*. *Parse* allows for the type to support conversion of a string to the UDT. For example, a UDT that represents a point (with *x* and *y* properties) could convert a string such as "2:5" to mean *x* = 2 and *y* = 5. The following code shows how, for this point UDT, to parse the *x* and *y* values from the string.

```
public static Point Parse(SqlString s)
{
    if (s.IsNull)
        return Point.Null;
    else
    {
        Point pt = new Point();
        String str = s.ToString();
        String[] xy = null;

        xy = str.Split(new Char[] { ':' }, 2);
        pt.x = System.Convert.ToInt32(xy[0]);
        pt.y = System.Convert.ToInt32(xy[1]);
        pt.is_Null = false;
        return (pt);
    }
}
```

This static method checks to see whether the string argument value is null and exits the procedure if it is. If it is not null, then it creates a new instance of the type and parses the *x* and *y* values accordingly. It then sets the value of the private variable *is_Null* to false, indicating that the type now has a value. And finally, it returns the type instance.

The UDT supports conversion back to a string by overriding the object's virtual *ToString* method. Many types in the .NET Framework do this, and *SqlTypes* are no exception. Using the point UDT example again, if *x* and *y* had values of 2 and 5, respectively, then the *ToString* method could return "2:5".

The following example demonstrates how null values are handled when converting to string. If the instance of this UDT is indeed null, this method simply returns the string "NULL". This is a stylistic choice—some developers prefer to return an empty string, and others like to put curly brackets around the word *null*, as in "{NULL}", to make sure it stands out when displayed with other data. The only recommendation I would make is to set a standard and use it consistently.

```
public override string ToString()
{
    if (this.IsNull)
        return "NULL";
```

```
else
    return this.m_x + ":" + this.m_y;
}
```

If the UDT doesn't conform to these rules, as before, the assembly will compile and can be registered in SQL Server. Because of this noncompliance, however, any attempt to register the UDT itself will throw an exception.

Constructors

A UDT requires a public zero-argument constructor. For classes, you can choose to write the zero-argument constructor yourself or let the compiler create it for you. For structs, you can't define a zero-argument constructor, so you must let the compiler create it.

A UDT can also have additional overloaded constructors that have, of course, at least one argument. Although they are not usable in TSQL, they can be used by other .NET consumers of this type, or within the type itself, as demonstrated in this code snippet:

```
private String m_string;
private Boolean is_null;
public MyType()
{
    m_string = "";
    is_null = true;
}
public MyType(String s)
{
    m_string = s;
    is_null = false;
}
public String MyString
{
    get
    {
        return m_string;
    }
    set
    {
        m_string = value;
        is_null = false;
    }
}
public static MyType Parse(SqlString s)
{
    MyType u;

    if (s.IsNull)
        u = new MyType();
    else
        u = new MyType((String) s);

    return u;
}
```

Although SQL Server 2005 can't take advantage of the constructor that takes a *String* argument, the *Parse* method certainly can—or, more accurately, any other .NET-based code can. The only drawback here is that constructors are the only public type member that can be overloaded. If you define a public, overloaded member, you will be able to compile the assembly and register it; and you will even be able to register the UDT itself. All will appear fine until you try to access the overloaded member, in which case, an exception will be thrown. So, if I added a public, overloaded method called *MyMethod*, as in

```
public Int32 MyMethod()
{
    return (Int32) m_string.Length;
}
public Int32 MyMethod(Int32 value)
{
    return (Int32) (m_string.Length + value);
}
```

attempting to execute

```
DECLARE @a MyType
SELECT @a.MyMethod()
```

in T-SQL, this would be the result:

```
.Net SqlClient Data Provider: Msg 6572, Level 16, State 1, Line 3
```

More than one method, property, or field was found with name *MyMethod* in class *MyType* in assembly *MyCLRProject1*. Overloaded methods, properties, or fields are not supported.

Properties and Methods

Although not required, a UDT usually will have at least one public property or field defined; it could avoid either of these two and instead expose a mutable public method (a method that can change a field value of the type). The UDT could even avoid all three of these and simply use the static *Parse* method (mentioned earlier in this section) to assign a value to a private field and use the *ToString* method to retrieve this value.

I point out all of these options for a reason: A UDT doesn't require any public fields, properties, or methods (outside of the ones previously mentioned for conversion and nullability). If, however, you want to have a viable UDT, as I already mentioned, you will likely define at least one public property.

I spent a lot of time investigating UDTs, trying various combinations of properties, methods, and fields, including none of these and all of these. I found that you could have a compilable, registerable UDT that was "usable" (I use the term loosely here) in TSQL if you create a struct in .NET that defines the bare minimum of required features for a UDT. This UDT is, at best, usable from a learning standpoint, but certainly not viable for real-world use. The following is my legal but totally impractical UDT called *Struct1*.

```
[Serializable]
[StructLayout(LayoutKind.Sequential)]
[SqlUserDefinedType(Format.Native)]
public struct Struct1: INullable
{
    public SqlInt32 MyInt32;
    public override string ToString()
    {
        return MyInt32.ToString();
    }
    public static Struct1 Parse(SqlString s)
    {
        Struct1 u = new Struct1();
        u.MyInt32 = (SqlInt32) System.Convert.ToInt32(s);
        return u;
    }
    public static Struct1 Null
    {
        get     {return new Struct1(); }
    }
    public Boolean IsNull
    {
        get {return MyInt32.IsNull;}
    }
}
```

Not only does this code compile, but it can be registered and used in SQL Server 2005 with ease. It has the ability to store a *SqlInt32* value in the public *MyInt32* field, can convert to and from a string, and knows when it is null. But why bother when there is already a data type that does all of this and more and is native to SQL Server? That's right, I'm talking about *Int*. Would I ever use a UDT like this one in production code? No. Would I use it as a teaching aid? Most definitely.

Although this example demonstrates how easy it can be to create a UDT in .NET, I don't mean to imply that designing and implementing a UDT design is simple. UDTs are by far more complex than the other CLR-based objects. This example, although viable, is far from practical. A truly viable UDT would have more complexity and would require more design consideration on the part of the developer. Later in this section, you'll see two additional UDTs, each more complex than the other (and both more complex than this example).

Fields and Properties

For all you .NET developers out there, during your development endeavors, you have likely created a struct or class that contains fields and/or possibly properties. Implementing these type members works the same in a UDT. Public fields and properties are usable by the type in TSQL. For example, if I created a UDT that represented a point, I might give it two fields, x and y, that represent the point's location, like so:

```
public Int32 x;
public Int32 y;
```

If I want to validate the point before accepting its value—perhaps only non-negative points are allowed by the UDT—I would want to use properties instead, as follows:

```
private Int32 m_x;
private Int32 m_y;
private Boolean is_Null;
public Int32 x
{
    get { return (this.m_x); }
    set
    {
        if (value < 0)
            this.m_y = 0;
        else
            this.m_y = value;
        this.is_Null = false;
    }
}
public Int32 y
{
    get { return (this.m_y); }
    set
    {
        if (value < 0)
            this.m_y = 0;
        else
            this.m_y = value;
        this.is_Null = false;
    }
}
```

In either case, the property would appear the same to the developer using the UDT in SQL Server 2005. The difference is in what you do behind the scenes in the property code. The preceding example not only shows the prevention of non-negative values (by setting the negative value to 0) but also assigns the *is_Null* variable a value of false, indicating that the UDT itself is no longer null.

The following example TSQL code shows the UDT being used. Either implementation (field or property) of x and y would work here.

```
DECLARE @p Point
SET @p.x = 3
SET @p.y = 4
SELECT SQRT(SQUARE(@p.x) + SQUARE(@p.y)) AS DistanceToHome
```

The last statement, which calculates the distance to point {0, 0}, could be implemented by the UDT itself—which brings me to the next topic.

Methods

UDTs can also have public methods defined for use by the TSQL developer using the UDT. If the *DistanceToHome* value that I calculated in TSQL in the preceding example is used with any frequency (more than once, really), the UDT should implement a method that does this work for you. You wonder why. Well, since the calculation is entirely mathematical and based on values in the UDT itself, the CLR can do this work faster than TSQL.

The following example is one possible implementation to calculate the distance of the point to location {0, 0}.

```
public decimal DistanceToHome()
{
    Point pt1 = this;

    if (pt1.IsNull)
        return (Decimal) 0;

    double xdiff = Convert.ToDouble(pt1.x);
    double ydiff = Convert.ToDouble(pt1.y);

    return System.Convert.ToDecimal(
        System.Math.Sqrt(System.Convert.ToDouble(
        (xdiff * xdiff) + (ydiff * ydiff))));
}
```

This example assumes that if the UDT is null, then it is at location {0, 0}, and thus it returns a distance of 0. If the UDT is not null, then the square root of the sum of the squares is calculated and returned. This method is trivial to create and accesses only field member information of the type. What if the method needs to change field member values? You're about to find out why all methods are not created equal.

Method Attributes

In typical .NET development, a method can either access or modify field values. These are known as, respectively, nonmutable and mutable methods. There is no preference as to which it does and no consequences to having a method perform reads only on field values (nonmutable) or be able to change field values (mutable).

In a UDT, you can also have methods return values based on the instance field values (nonmutable) or can even modify these instance field values (mutable). But unlike typical .NET development, creating a mutable method has consequences. For a UDT to have a mutable method defined, the method must state to SQL Server that it can be mutable. It does this via the *IsMutator* property, one of several properties that can be assigned in the *SqlMethod* attribute.

SqlMethod is an optional attribute that allows the developer to specify special features of a method. *IsMutator* is one of four properties of this attribute. It is false by default, and it must be specified and set to true if the method needs to modify the instance. Another property, *Deterministic*, also *Boolean* and false by default, marks the method as being deterministic (true) or nondeterministic (false). Deterministic methods guarantee that the value returned will always be the same for the same argument values. For example, the *Square* function is deterministic; if passed an argument of 2, it will always return a value of 4. *GetDate*, on the other hand, is nondeterministic; even with no arguments, it can return a different value every time it is called.

OnNullCall is the third property and, like the others, is *Boolean*, but unlike them, is true by default. If *OnNullCall* is false, then if any of the method argument values are null, the method will not evaluate and simply return null, regardless of other argument values. If true, the method always evaluates, even if all the argument values are null. And finally, the *DataAccess* property states whether or not the method includes SQL SELECT statements. It can be set to either *DataAccessKind.None* (the default) or *DataAccessKind.Read*. I'll cover *DataAccess* in more depth later in this chapter.

These attribute properties are not for the benefit of the UDT developer but rather for the benefit of SQL Server. The more SQL Server knows about the type, the more efficiently it can use the type. All of these attribute properties default as indicated, so even if they are not specified in the type code, SQL Server "knows" their respective values just the same.

The Point Struct UDT

You have now read about what is involved in creating a UDT; this first example demonstrates how to implement a struct as a UDT in SQL Server 2005. It contains all the features I've mentioned up to this point, including two properties and one method. It also has previously unmentioned items that I will go over after the code listing.

```
using System;
using System.Data.SqlTypes;
using System.Data.SqlServer;
using System.Data.Sql;
namespace Wintellect.SQLServer.UDT
{
    [Serializable]
    [SqlUserDefinedType(Format.Native)]
    public struct Point: INullable
```

```
{
    private Boolean is_Null;
    private Int32 m_x;
    private Int32 m_y;
    public Boolean IsNull
    {
        get { return (is_Null); }
    }
    public static Point Null
    {
        get
        {
            Point pt = new Point();
            return (pt);
        }
    }
    public override string ToString()
    {
        if (this.IsNull)
            return "NULL";
        else
            return this.m_x + ":" + this.m_y;
    }

    public static Point Parse(SqlString s)
    {
        if (s.IsNull)
            return Point.Null;
        else
        {
            Point pt = new Point();
            String str = s.ToString();
            String[] xy = null;

            xy = str.Split(new Char[] { ':' }, 2);
            pt.x = System.Convert.ToInt32(xy[0]);
            pt.y = System.Convert.ToInt32(xy[1]);
            pt.is_Null = false;
            return (pt);
        }
    }

    public Int32 x
    {
        get { return (this.m_x); }
        set
        {
            this.m_x = value;
            this.is_Null = false;
        }
    }
    public Int32 y
    {
        get { return (this.m_y); }
        set
```

```
            {
                this.m_y = value;
                this.is_Null = false;
            }
        }

        public decimal DistanceTo(object other)
        {
            Point pt2 = (Point)other;
            Point pt1 = this;

            if (pt1.IsNull)
            {
                pt1.x = 0;
                pt1.y = 0;
            }

            if (pt2.IsNull)
            {
                pt2.x = 0;
                pt2.y = 0;
            }

            double xdiff = Convert.ToDouble(pt1.x - pt2.x);
            double ydiff = Convert.ToDouble(pt1.y - pt2.y);

            return System.Convert.ToDecimal(
                System.Math.Sqrt(System.Convert.ToDouble(
                (xdiff * xdiff) + (ydiff * ydiff))));
        }
    }
}
```

Although I haven't used any namespace references in other sample code, I did want to point out the effect of using it. When registering the UDT in TSQL, if a namespace is specified for the type, the namespace must be referenced in the CREATE TYPE statement, as shown here:

```
CREATE TYPE Point EXTERNAL NAME MyUDTs:[Wintellect.SQLServer.UDT.Point]
```

Without the namespace, it would be a more simplified version, like this:

```
CREATE TYPE Point EXTERNAL NAME MyUDTs:Point
```

Tip   Should you use namespaces in creating your code? Yes. Using namespaces lets you organize your code in a hierarchical fashion. It also helps prevent the chance for name and type collisions. And although SQL Server 2005 unfortunately does not take advantage of this feature, other .NET code that references your .NET-based objects in SQL Server 2005 does.

I also want to point out something regarding the private field, *is_Null*. Since this is a struct, no public zero-argument constructor can be defined. Normally, the purpose of such a constructor is to default field values, and in this case, *is_Null* needs to be defaulted to true. Otherwise, if the *IsNull* property is accessed immediately after declaring a variable of this type in TSQL, it will return a value of false when it should be returning a value of true.

```
DECLARE @a Point
SET @a.x = 1
IF @a IS NULL
    PRINT 'null'
ELSE
    PRINT 'not null'

IF @a.IsNull = 1
    PRINT 'null'
ELSE
    PRINT 'not null'
```

If you run this batch, it should display "not null" twice, and indeed it does. If the SET statement on the second line is removed, however, this batch will display the string "null" then "not null". This result stems from the fact that the *IsNull* property will have a value of false (0) because private field *is_Null* is never initialized, even if @a is indeed null. This is a problem, but fortunately, it is easily corrected. If I make one small change to the *Null* property, I can get the *IsNull* property to behave correctly. Take a look at this modified version of the *Null* property:

```
public static Point Null
{
    get
    {
        Point pt = new Point();
        pt.is_Null = true; //added this line of code
        return (pt);
    }
}
```

Because of this one little line of code in the static *Null* property, the UDT now behaves as expected. Using the preceding TSQL example, it will return "null" twice, as you would want it to. Why? Since the variable is declared to be of type *Point*, and it is not assigned a value, SQL Server knows that the variable itself is null. When the line in TSQL that requests the *IsNull* property is executed, there is no instance of the type because it is null, so SQL Server calls the static *Null* method to get an instance of the type for the purpose of being able to evaluate the *IsNull* property. This new *Null* property returns an instance of *Point*, but only after setting that instance's *is_Null* field value to true.

When I finally understood this functionality, I smiled. Before I realized exactly what was happening, I was finding it difficult to justify using structs for UDTs because I had no means of defaulting this one value that needs to be defaulted. There are other ways to get around this issue, but to me, this was certainly the most elegant.

The Email Struct UDT

This second example also demonstrates how to implement a struct as a UDT in SQL Server 2005, but this time with a bit more complexity. This example additionally demonstrates the *UserDefined* serialization format and implements the *IBinarySerialize* interface and its *Write* and *Read* methods. The only reason I don't use *Native* is because the address field is a *String* type, which, as I noted earlier, precludes the UDT from using this serialization format.

This UDT also implements the *IComparable* interface, which has a single public method, *CompareTo*, that accepts an object as its sole argument and returns an *Int32* indicating whether the instance is less than (-1), greater than (1), or equal to (0) the argument to which it is being compared.

This UDT also demonstrates how to override other virtual methods, such as *Object's GetHashCode* and *Equals* methods.

```
using System;
using System.Data.SqlTypes;
using System.Data.SqlServer;
using System.Data.Sql;
using System.Text.RegularExpressions;
[Serializable]
[SqlUserDefinedType
    (Format.UserDefined, MaxByteSize = 122, IsByteOrdered = true)]
public struct Email: INullable, IComparable, IBinarySerialize
{
    private bool is_Null;
    private string m_address;
    #region INullable Members
    public bool IsNull
    {
        get {return (is_Null);}
    }
    public static Email Null
    {
        get
        {
            Email email = new Email();
            email.is_Null = true;
            return (email);
        }
    }
    #endregion
    #region String Conversion Members
    public override string ToString ()
```

```csharp
{
    if (this.IsNull)
        return "NULL";
    else
        return (this.m_address);
}
public static Email Parse(SqlString s)
{
    if (s.IsNull)
        return Email.Null;
    else
    {
        Email email = new Email();
        string str = Convert.ToString(s);
        try
        {
            email.Address = str;
        }
        catch (ArgumentException aex)
        {
            throw aex;
        }
        return (email);
    }
}
#endregion
#region Class Properties
public string Address
{
    get {return (this.m_address);}
    set
    {
        if (value.Length <= 120 && Regex.IsMatch(value,
            @"^([\w-]+\.)*?[\w-]+@[\w-]+\.([\w-]+\.)*?[\w]+$",
            RegexOptions.IgnoreCase))
        {
            this.m_address = value;
            this.is_Null = false;
        }
        else
        {
            throw new ArgumentException(
                "Specified email address is not valid.",
                "Address");
        }
    }
}
#endregion
#region Class Methods
public string NoSpamAddress()
{
    return ("RemoveSpam-" + this.m_address);
}
public string Name()
```

```csharp
        {
            return (this.m_address.Substring(0, this.m_address.IndexOf("@")));
        }
        public string Location()
        {
            return (this.m_address.Substring(this.m_address.IndexOf("@")+ 1));
        }
        public override bool Equals (object other)
        {
            return this.CompareTo (other) == 0;
        }
        public override int GetHashCode ()
        {
            if (this.IsNull)
                return 0;
            return this.ToString().GetHashCode ();
        }
        #endregion
        #region IComparable Members
        public int CompareTo (object other)
        {
            if (other == null)
                return 1;
            Email email = (Email) other;
            if (this.IsNull)
            {
                if (email.IsNull)
                    return 0;
                return -1;
            }
            if (email.IsNull)
                return 1;
            return this.ToString().CompareTo(email.ToString());
        }
        #endregion
        #region IBinarySerialize Members
        public void Write (System.IO.BinaryWriter w)
        {
            byte header = (byte)(this.IsNull ? 1 : 0);
            w.Write (header);
            if (header == 1)
                return;
            w.Write(this.m_address.PadRight(120, (char)0));
        }
        public void Read (System.IO.BinaryReader r)
        {
            byte header = r.ReadByte();
            if (header == 1)
            {
                this.is_Null = true;
                return;
            }
            this.is_Null = false;
            this.m_address = r.ReadString().TrimEnd(new char[] {(char)0});
        }
        #endregion
    }
```

Once again, I'd like to discuss a few items from the code listing. Although a lot of what is here is essentially the same as what you saw in the Point UDT example, there are a few twists here that make this UDT not only more interesting but also more efficient than its Point predecessor.

The first tidbit for discussion is the code in the *Parse* method. It takes the *SqlString*, casts it to a *String*, and then sends it to the *Address* property. The *Address* property set accessor does the validation and throws an exception if the email is invalid. If this does occur, the *Parse* method simply rethrows the exception. In my first version of this struct, I was validating the email address in the set accessor of the *Address* property but was neglecting to do so in the *Parse* method.

> Tip   Be sure that all members that allow field modification follow the same validation rules. For example, have the *Parse* method use the public properties to set the field data to ensure that the validation is occurring. Any mutable method should also follow this rule.

The real feature I want to talk about is the increase in efficiency. This UDT was designed so that it could be indexed based not on any property or field values but rather on the raw serialized bytes. To achieve this, I had to do a few special things here and there in the code. The first was to set the *IsByteOrdered* property to true in the *SqlUserDefinedType* attribute. This tells SQL Server that I intend to use the raw serialized bytes for comparisons and ordering.

Since I want the raw byte order to be equivalent to the alphabetic ordering of the email address as a string, I will need to write the bytes out in such a way that they guarantee the correct order. Normally, I would have written the *Write* method of the *BinaryWriter* like this:

```
w.Write(this.m_address);
```

The problem with this is the way that the *Write* method writes strings. It prefixes the data with the length of the string and then puts the byte data for the string. If you were to sort on the raw byte data, the data derived from the shortest strings would always come first because the first byte would be the length of the string. So, the email address *"you@somecompany.com"* would look like this in raw byte data:

```
0x0013796F7540736F6D65636F6D70616E792E636F6D
```

The first byte, 0x00, is the flag indicating the value is not null. The next byte, 0x13, is the length (19) of the email address. If another email started with the letter *a* but was a longer address, its second byte would be greater than 0x13 and would sort after this email that starts with the letter *y*.

How do you fix this problem? Pad the results such that all email addresses are the same length when serialized. This would guarantee the second byte to be the same for all email addresses. You do this by padding the right side of the string with the null character. The new line is written as follows:

```
w.Write(this.m_address.PadRight(120, (char)0));
```

Now because of this padding, *BinaryReader* needs to "unpad" the results when deserializing the data. When reading the string, I simply trimmed off the null characters.

```
this.m_address = r.ReadString().TrimEnd(new char[] {(char)0});
```

And now that I can guarantee the byte order to be the same as the semantic ordering of the email (alphabetically by address), what good does it do me? Well, because of the way this UDT is being implemented, it can be used as an index in its raw form. Which means that it could be used as a primary key field of a table. Which means that it can participate in a relationship to another table. Since the raw serialized bytes of the UDT are used for comparison, it is as efficient as any other data type when used as a primary key field or in comparison operations. Thus, if the UDT is used in an ORDER BY clause, it performs additionally also as well as a *Char* field of equivalent length (in this case, 122 bytes).

Using a UDT

In the process of talking about UDTs, I've already demonstrated several examples in TSQL. The following example TSQL code shows a variety of things, starting with the registration of the assembly and type. It is followed by a table that uses the UDT for its last column. A stored procedure that inserts data into this table is shown next, followed by an example of its use. Data is then selected from the table, including the UDT column. To wrap things up, the UDT column is modified via an UPDATE statement.

```
CREATE ASSEMBLY MyUDTs
FROM 'C:\Projects\SQLServer2005\UDTs\bin\Debug\MyUDTs.dll'
GO
CREATE TYPE Email EXTERNAL NAME MyUDTs: Email
GO
CREATE TABLE Membership
(UserID Int IDENTITY(1, 1) PRIMARY KEY NOT NULL,
UserName Nvarchar(32) NOT NULL,
EmailAddress Email NULL)
GO
CREATE PROCEDURE prAddUser
    @UserName Nvarchar(32),
    @EmailAddress Nvarchar(120)
AS
INSERT INTO Membership (UserName, Password, EmailAddress)
VALUES (@UserName, CAST(@EmailAddress AS Email))
GO
```

```
EXEC prAddUser 'peter', 'secret', 'peterdebetta@wintellect.com'

SELECT UserName, EmailAddress.Address
FROM Membership
WHERE UserID = 1

UPDATE Membership
SET EmailAddress.Address = 'peter.debetta@wintellect.com'
WHERE UserID = 1
```

You've now seen an example of using a UDT in variable declarations and table column definitions. UDTs can be used like other data types in SQL Server. The big difference is how you "speak" to the UDT. In many cases, you convert from a string data type or you must reference a property of the UDT. And just for kicks, let's update that email address one more time using yet another method:

```
DECLARE @email Email
SET @email.Address = 'peter.debetta@wintellect.com'

UPDATE Membership
SET EmailAddress = @email
WHERE UserID = 1
```

This last example shows the use of a variable of type *Email* being used to update the column of type *Email* in the table. Beautiful stuff!

A Word of Caution

Because UDTs can mimic table structure, I fear that many developers will become overzealous in their use of them within a database. UDTs are not meant to replace table structures but to add complex elements to a table design that would be difficult to implement in a table or that have complexity in logic for assignment of values.

One example that I will be discussing in a moment is an email UDT. This type is an excellent example of the proper use of a UDT. Sure, the email address could be easily represented as a *varchar* (or *nvarchar*, say) field, but the UDT takes things a step further and has built-in validation while maintaining equivalent performance to the native field type of *varchar* et al. It can be indexed and compared without having to invoke the CLR code base because it is comparable based on the raw binary storage of the data. This means that indexing and ordering the type, for example, works as efficiently as it would for a native type. And to top it off, it even has methods that will return the user name or mail server name from the email address and a method that returns a spam-prevention email address. To do that with a *varchar*, you would need to create a separate constraint and three additional user-defined functions.

My point in talking about all of this is to clarify that not everything belongs in a UDT. For example, you may be thinking that an Employee would be a great UDT object. It would have properties to represent employee attributes such as name, address, manager, pay scale, and so on. By encompassing all of these fields into a single type, you would lose the ability to compare the raw data of the field, indexing would be more difficult to implement because you would have to create computed columns on each of the properties or methods that you would want to index, each property value would have to be extracted via a property or method call, and all in all, things would not perform as well. Instead of creating a type to represent an employee, a better choice would be to create a type for certain attributes, like the employee's Social Security number (which could be encrypted in the database if a UDT is used), the employee's name, or as in the preceding example, the employee's email address.

Try not to overengineer UDTs. As I stated earlier, they are not replacements for table structures but rather are for smaller structures within tables. You're not going to revolutionize database development by trying to create an object-oriented database via UDTs.

There are always exceptions to rules, so don't be so cautious that you try to avoid UDTs. I can think of an excellent table structure that would consist of two fields, one of which is a UDT. Perhaps you have user configuration data that you want to persist in the database so a user's configuration will be available anywhere that the application is used. Configuration data can consist of several settings, including a color scheme, last search string, and so forth. A UDT, perhaps named Configuration, could be created to hold all of these config values. This Configuration UDT could then used in a table as follows:

```
CREATE TABLE UserConfiguration
(
    UserID Int NOT NULL,
    UserConfig Configuration NOT NULL
)
```

None of the property or method values will be accessed within SQL Server. This Configuration will not be indexed and it will not be compared to another Configuration. This UDT will exist solely for use in the client code that is talking to SQL Server. Therefore, there is no reason why this shouldn't be created as a UDT. In the next chapter, you'll learn that when a UDT exists as a type in SQL Server, the client sees the type in its .NET code as a native type. This reason, in addition to the reasons just stated, makes it very advantageous to employ a UDT to store these configuration values.

Summary

I know that developers are chomping at the bit to create stored procedures and functions in languages such as C#. Whereas many developers are looking to stored procedures and user-defined functions to change the way in which they implement business rules, I see UDTs playing just as big a role here, too. I suspect that few developers will really go more than surface deep into UDTs, partially because of a lack of interest and partially because of the inherent complexity they can introduce into a database. And it's a shame, because I see the UDT as the most powerful, albeit complex, feature of all the CLR integration features.

And to tell you the truth, it would take many more chapters to write about all the nuances of UDTs. But being that this book intends to introduce many development features instead of concentrating on any single feature, I will stop discussing UDTs and their use within SQL Server right now.

Appendix B
Longhorn

This appendix contains a chapter from *Introducing WinFX: The Application Programming Interface for the Next Generation of Microsoft Windows Code Name "Longhorn"* by Brent Rector (Microsoft Press, 2004). This title provides an introduction to the next generation Windows client operating system. Note that this product is still in development and, therefore, you can expect there will be changes in the finished product.

Chapter 4 Storage

In some ways, *personal computer* is an inadequate name. Most people don't use a personal computer to compute. They use a computer to communicate (through e-mail or instant messaging) and to store and organize their personal data (such as e-mail, documents, pictures, and digital music). Unfortunately, while your computer presently stores this data quite well, it does a relatively poor job of allowing you to organize the information so that you can find it later.

Disk capacity has been growing at roughly 70 percent annually over the last decade. It's presently possible to buy drives with more than 250 gigabytes (GB) of storage. It's likely that 500-GB drives will become available in the next few years and that many systems will have more than one disk drive. I just did a quick check on the computer on which I'm writing this chapter, and I have 283,667 files in 114,129 folders in only 200 GB of disk space. When I forget exactly where I put a file, it can take quite a while to find it again. In the worst case, I have to search the entire contents of each disk. In a few years, people will be able to store millions of files, most of which, if nothing improves, they'll never see again.

One reason people have difficulty finding information on their computer is because of the limited ability for the user to organize data. The present file system support for folders and files worked well originally because it was a familiar paradigm to most people and the number of files was relatively small. However, it doesn't easily allow you to store an image of your coworker Bob playing softball at the 2007 company picnic at a local park and later find the image when searching for documents that

- Mention Bob
- Involve sports
- Relate to company events
- Pertain to the park or its surrounding area
- Were created in 2007

The hierarchical folder structure doesn't work well when you want to categorize data in numerous ways. Therefore, we have a problem today in that we have lots of stuff to store and no good way to categorize it. In addition to categorizing information, which many people associate with attaching a fixed set of keywords to data, people need to relate data. For example, I might want to relate a picture to the company picnic, or I might want to relate a picture to Bob, who is also a member of an organization to which I donate time and effort, as a contact.

Another problem is that we store the same stuff in multiple places in multiple formats. Developers spend much time and effort creating their own unique storage abstractions for everyday information such as People, Places, Times, and Events. For example, Microsoft Outlook has a definition of a Contact. The Microsoft Windows Address Book also has its own definition of a contact. Each instant messaging application has yet another. Each application stores its definition of a contact in a unique, isolated silo of information.

There are a number of problems with current approaches to data storage, including the following:

- Developers reinvent the basic data abstractions repeatedly.

- Multiple applications cannot easily share common data.

- The same information lives in multiple locations.

- The user repeatedly enters the same information.

- Separate copies of data become unsynchronized.

- There are no notifications of data change.

What Is WinFS?

WinFS is the new storage system in Longhorn. It improves the Microsoft Windows platform in three ways. First, it allows you to categorize your information in multiple ways and relate one item of information to another. Second, it provides a common storage format for information collected on an everyday basis, such as information dealing with people, places, images, and more. Third, it promotes data sharing of common information across multiple applications from multiple vendors.

WinFS Is a Storage Platform

WinFS is an active storage platform for organizing, searching for, and sharing all kinds of information. This platform defines a rich data model that allows you to use and define rich data types that the storage platform can use. WinFS contains numerous schemas that describe real entities such as Images, Documents, People, Places, Events,

Tasks, and Messages. These entities can be quite complex. For example, a person can have multiple names, multiple physical and e-mail addresses, a current location, and much more.

Independent software vendors (ISVs) can also define their own new data types and provide their schema to WinFS. By allowing WinFS to manage complex storage problems, an ISV can concentrate on developing its unique application logic and leverage the richer storage facilities of WinFS for its everyday and custom data.

WinFS contains a relational engine that allows you to locate instances of storage types by using powerful, relational queries. WinFS allows you to combine these storage entities in meaningful ways using relationships. One contact can be a member of the Employee group of an Organization while concurrently a member of the Household group for a specific address. ISVs automatically gain the ability to search, replicate, secure, and establish relationships among their unique data types as well as among the predefined Windows data types.

This structure allows the user to pose questions to the system and ask it to locate information rather than asking the system to individually search folders. For example, you can ask WinFS to find all e-mail messages from people on your instant messenger buddy list for which you don't have a phone number. Using relational queries, you can find all members of a Household for a particular employee with a birthday in the current month.

WinFS also supports multiple flexible programming models that allow you to choose the appropriate application programming interface (API) for the task. You can access the store by using traditional relational queries using structured query language (SQL). Alternatively, you can use .NET classes and objects to access the data store. You can also use XML-based APIs on the data store. WinFS also supports data access through the traditional Microsoft Win32 file system API. You can even mix and match—that is, use multiple APIs for a single task. However, for most purposes, developers will use the managed class APIs to change data in the WinFS store. It will often be far more complex to make an update using raw SQL statements as compared to using the object APIs.

In addition, WinFS provides a set of data services for monitoring, managing, and manipulating your data. You can register to receive events when particular data items change. You can schedule WinFS to replicate your data to other systems.

WinFS Is a File System

For traditional file-based data, such as text documents, audio tracks, and video clips, WinFS is the new Windows file system. Typically, you will store the main data of a file, the file stream, as a file on an NTFS volume. However, whenever you call an API that changes or adds items with NTFS file stream parts, WinFS extracts the metadata from the stream and adds the metadata to the WinFS store. This metadata describes information about the stream, such as its path, plus any information that WinFS can extract from the stream. Depending on file contents, this metadata can be the author (of a document), the genre (of an audio file), keywords (from a PDF file), and more. WinFS synchronizes the NTFS-resident file stream and the WinFS-resident metadata. New Longhorn applications can also choose to store their file streams directly in WinFS. File streams can be accessed using the existing Win32 file system API or the new WinFS API.

WinFS Isn't Just a File System

A file system manages files and folders. While WinFS does manage files and folders, it also manages all types of nonfile-based data, such as personal contacts, event calendars, tasks, and e-mail messages. WinFS data can be structured, semistructured, or unstructured. Structured data includes a schema that additionally defines what the data is for and how you should use it. Because WinFS is, in part, a relational system, it enforces data integrity with respect to semantics, transactions, and constraints.

WinFS isn't just a relational system, either. It supports both hierarchical storage and relational storage. It supports returning data as structured types and as objects—types plus behavior. You might consider WinFS a hierarchical, relational, object-oriented data storage system—although it actually contains certain aspects of each of those traditional storage systems. WinFS extends beyond the traditional file system and relational database system. It is the store for all types of data on the newest Windows platform.

WinFS and NTFS

You can store a file either in the traditional NTFS file system or in the new WinFS data store just like you can store things in FAT32 or on CD-ROMs or in NTFS today. Normally, a file stored in NTFS is not visible in WinFS. Longhorn applications using the new WinFS APIs can access data stored either in WinFS or in NTFS. In addition, Longhorn applications can continue to use the Win32 API to access data stored in the NTFS file system.

File Promotion

Files are either in WinFS or not. Any item that has a file stream part can participate in promotion/demotion, which we more generally call *metadata handling*. When WinFS promotes a file, it extracts the metadata from the known NTFS file content and adds the metadata to the WinFS data store. The actual data stream of the file remains in the NTFS file system. You can then query WinFS regarding the metadata as if the file natively resides within WinFS. WinFS also detects changes in the NTFS file and updates the metadata within the WinFS data store as necessary.

File Import and Export

You can also import a file to WinFS from NTFS and export a file from WinFS to NTFS. Importing and exporting a file moves both the file content and the metadata. After importing or exporting, the new file is completely independent of the original file.

WinFS Programming Model

The WinFS programming model includes data access, data manipulation, WinFS data class extensibility, data synchronization, data change notifications, and event prioritization. Data access and data manipulation allow you to create, retrieve, update, and delete data stored within WinFS and to exercise domain-specific behaviors. Data class extensibility enables you to extend WinFS schemas with custom fields and custom types. Data synchronization allows you to synchronize data between WinFS stores and between a WinFS and a non-WinFS store.

The top of the WinFS data model hierarchy is a WinFS *service*, which is simply an instance of WinFS. One level in the hierarchy from the service is a *volume*. A volume is the largest autonomous container of items. Each WinFS instance contains one or more volumes. Within a volume are *items*.

WinFS introduces the item as the new unit of consistency and operation, rather than the file. The storage system stores items. You have rich query ability over items. An item is effectively a base type of the storage system. An item therefore has a set of data attributes and provides a basic query capability.

People typically organize data in the real world according to some system that makes sense in a given domain. All such systems partition data into named groups. WinFS models this notion with the concept of a *folder*. A folder is a special type of item. There are two types of folders: *containment folders* and *virtual folders*.

A containment folder is an item that contains holding links to other items and models the common concept of a file system folder. An item exists as long as at least one holding link references it. Note that a containment folder doesn't directly contain the items logically present in the folder but instead contains links to those items. This allows multiple containment folders to *contain* the same item.

A virtual folder is a dynamic collection of items. It is a named set of items. You can either enumerate the set explicitly or specify a query that returns the members of the set. A virtual folder specified by a query is quite interesting. When you add a new item to the store that meets the criteria of the query for a virtual folder, the new item is automatically a member of the virtual folder. A virtual folder is itself an item. Conceptually, it represents a set of nonholding links to items, as you can see in Figure 4-1.

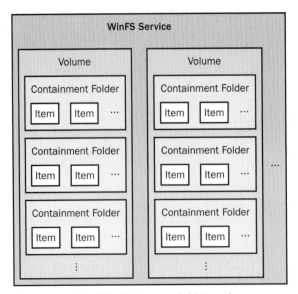

Figure 4-1   The WinFS data model hierarchy

Sometimes, you need to model a highly constrained notion of containment—for example, a Microsoft Word document embedded in an e-mail message is, in a sense, bound more tightly to its container than, for example, a file contained within a folder. WinFS expresses this notion by using *embedded items*. An embedded item is a special kind of link within an item (named Embedded Link) that references another item. The referenced item can be bound to or otherwise manipulated only within the context of the containing item.

Finally, WinFS provides the notion of *categories* as a way to classify items. You can associate one or more categories with every item in WinFS. WinFS, in effect, tags the category name onto the item. You can then specify the category name in searches. The WinFS data model allows the definition of a hierarchy of categories, thus enabling a tree-like classification of data.

Organizing Information

All these features together allow five ways to organize your information in WinFS:

- **Hierarchical folder-based organization**   With this approach, you still have the traditional hierarchical folder and item organization structure. All items in a WinFS data store must reside in a container, and one of these container types is a folder.

- **Type-based organization**   An item is always of a particular type. For example, you have Person items, Photo items, Organization items, and many other available types. You can even create new types and store them in the WinFS data store.

- **Item property–based organization**   You can view items that have one or more properties set to specified values. This is, in effect, a virtual folder view with a query that returns the items with the specified value for the specified properties.

- **Relationship-based organization**   You can retrieve items based on their relationship to other items—for example, a Person can be a member of an Organization, and either one can be organized or searched for in terms of this relationship.

- **Category-based organization**   You can create and associate any number of user-defined keywords with an item. Subsequently you can retrieve the items that have a specific value for an associated keyword. You won't, however, be able to create categorization taxonomies, so this organization technique is not as powerful as the preceding approaches.

WinFS APIs

WinFS provides three data access APIs: the managed WinFS API, the ADO.NET API, and the Win32 API. The WinFS API is a strongly typed "high level" API. ADO.NET provides a lower level API for working with data as XML or as tables or rows. Using ADO.NET, you can access data stored in WinFS by using Transact-Structured Query Language (T-SQL) and, when you want, retrieve data in XML using the T-SQL's FOR XML capability. The Win32 API allows access to the files and folders stored in WinFS.

You might prefer to use multiple access patterns to solve a problem. For example, you can issue a T-SQL query that returns a set of contacts as managed objects of the WinFS Contact type. Regardless of the API you use, each API ultimately manipulates data in the WinFS store using T-SQL.

In many cases, you will prefer to use the managed WinFS API. These .NET Framework classes automatically perform the object-relationship mapping needed to translate between object-oriented programming constructs, and they perform the necessary T-SQL to achieve the WinFS data access.

Using the Managed WinFS Classes

The WinFS managed classes reside in the *System.Storage* namespace and its nested namespaces. Many applications will also use WinFS type definitions from the *System.Storage.Core* namespace. You can additionally use types from more specialized namespaces. For example, the managed classes that manipulate the system definition of a Contact reside in the *System.Storage.Contact* namespace. For simplicity, all the code examples in this chapter will use the following set of *using* declarations:

```
using System.Storage;
using System.Storage.Core;
using System.Storage.Contact;
```

ItemContext

The WinFS store consists of items organized into folders and categorized. The first step in working with WinFS is to identify the set of items with which you want to work. We call this process *binding*, and the set of items can be any of the following:

- An entire volume (also known as the *root folder*)
- An identifiable subset of items in a given volume—for example, a particular containment folder or virtual folder
- An individual item
- A WinFS share (which identifies a volume, a folder, a virtual folder, or an individual item)

To bind to a set of items, you create a *System.Storage.ItemContext* object and connect it to a WinFS data store. Use the static *System.Storage.ItemContext.Open* helper method to create an *ItemContext* object.

The following code creates an *ItemContext* that connects to the default local WinFS volume. The default is the *local-computer-name*\DefaultStore share:

```
System.Storage.ItemContext ctx = System.Storage.ItemContext.Open ();
...
ctx.Close();
```

Alternatively, you can pass a string to the constructor to connect the item context to a specific WinFS store. The following code creates an item context connected to a WinFS share identified by the \\machine\Legal Documents share:

```
ItemContext ctx = null;
try {
ctx = ItemContext.Open (@"\machine\Legal Documents");
    ...
}
finally {
  if (ctx != null) ctx.Dispose();
}
```

Be sure to close or dispose of the context object as soon as you finish using it regardless of exceptions. An *ItemContext* uses significant unmanaged resources—such as a connection to the store—that you should free up in a timely manner. To make closing contexts as convenient as possible, the *ItemContext* class implements the *IDisposable* interface. Therefore, you can use the C# *using* statement as shown in the following example to release these resources:

```
using (ItemContext ctx = ItemContext.Open (@"D:\MyStore")) {
    ...
}
```

Storing a New Item in a WinFS Data Store

Every item in a WinFS data store must be a member of a folder of the store. You obtain the root of the folder hierarchy by calling the extremely well-named static method *System.Storage.Folder.GetRootFolder*. However, there are also several system-defined containers for storing application-specific data. You often use one of the static methods on the *UserDataFolder* class to retrieve a folder in which you then place new items.

Getting a Folder

In the following example, I'll find the current user's Personal Contacts folder if it exists and create it when it doesn't exist. Note that this is a somewhat contrived example—the system automatically creates a user's Personal Contacts folder if it doesn't exist when the user first logs into a system—but it gives me a chance to show how to create an expected folder when it doesn't exist.

```
ItemContext ctx = ItemContext.Open ();
WellKnownFolder contactsFolder =
        UserDataFolder.FindUsersWellKnownFolderWithType (ctx,
                    GeneralCategories.PersonalContactsFolder);

if (contactsFolder == null) {
    //create the Personal Contacts folder
    Folder userDataFolder = UserDataFolder.FindMyUserDataFolder (ctx);
    WellKnownFolder subFolder = new WellKnownFolder (ctx);
    CategoryRef category = new CategoryRef (ctx,
                        GeneralCategories.PersonalContactsFolder);

    // Associate the PersonalContactsFolder category to the folder
    subFolder.FolderType = category;
    userDataFolder.AddMember (subFolder);
    ctx.Update();
}
```

The preceding code does a number of interesting things. First, I try to locate an existing folder contained in the user's personal data folder hierarchy. I'm not looking for the folder by a well-known name. Instead, I'm locating the folder within the user's personal data tree that has previously been associated with the well-known category *PersonalContactsFolder*. The shell displays this folder when you select My Contacts.

This folder normally already exists, but when it doesn't, I retrieve the root folder for the user's data hierarchy. I create a new item, of type *WellKnownFolder*, and then create a reference to a well-known category—the *PersonalContactsFolder* category. I then set the type of the new folder to the *PersonalContactsFolder* category type, and finally, I add the new folder to its containing folder—the user's personal data root folder. WinFS doesn't save any changes to the data store until you call *Update* on the item context (which I regularly forget to do).

Of course, this is the verbose way to find the Personal Contacts folder. I wanted to show you how things work. Normally, I'd use the following code instead. The *Find-MyPersonalContactsFolder* method finds the existing folder.

```
WellKnownFolder userDataFolder =
        UserDataFolder.FindMyPersonalContactsFolder (ctx);
```

Creating a New Item

As I now have the Personal Contacts folder, it seems appropriate to create a new contact in the folder. In the following example, I'll create a number of Person contacts and add them to the folder:

```
Person[] CreateFriends (ItemContext ctx) {
  string[] GivenNames = { "Monica", "Rachel", "Chandler",
                          "Joey",   "Phoebe", "Ross"};
  string[] SurNames = { "Uchra",    "Emerald", "Ranier",
                        "Fibonacci", "Smorgasbord", "Uchra"};
  Person[] Friends = new Person [GivenNames.Length];

  for (int index = 0; index < GivenNames.Length; index++) {
    string linkName = GivenNames[index] + " " + SurNames[index];
    Person p = Person.CreatePersonalContact (ctx, linkName);
    Friends[index] = p;

    p.DisplayName = linkName;
    FullName fn = p.GetPrimaryName ();
    fn.GivenName = GivenNames[index];
    fn.Surname = SurNames[index];
  }
  ctx.Update ();
}
```

The prior code uses the static *Person.CreatePersonalContact* method. This method

- Creates a new Person item in the specified item context

- Creates a new *FolderMember* relationship with the specified name that references the Person

- Adds the *FolderMember* relationship to the *PersonalContactsFolder*'s *Relationship* collection

I subsequently update the *DisplayName*, *GivenName*, and *Surname* properties of the Person item. As always, I call *Update* on the item context to save the changes to the data store.

Let's look more closely at the *CreatePersonalContact* method. It is equivalent to the following:

```
// Find the PersonalContacts folder
WellKnownFolder contactsFolder =
        UserDataFolder.FindUsersWellKnownFolderWithType (ctx,
                        GeneralCategories.PersonalContactsFolder);
// Create a new Person item
Person p = new Person (ctx);

// Need a folder relationship that references the new Person
FolderMember fm = new FolderMember (p, linkName);  folder.Relationships.Add (fm);
ctx.Update ();
```

Relationship Items

WinFS defines a relationship data model that allows you to relate items to one another. When you define the schema for a data type, you can define zero or more relationships as part of the schema. For example, the Folder schema defines the *FolderMember* relationship. The Organization schema defines the *Employee* relationship. For each such defined relationship, there is a class that represents the relationship itself. This class is derived from the *Relationship* class and contains members specific to the relationship type. There is also a strongly typed "virtual" collection class. This class is derived from *VirtualRelationshipCollection* and allows relationship instances to be created and deleted.

A relationship relates a source item to a target item. In the previous example, the Personal Contacts folder was the source item and the Person item was the target item. The *FolderMember* relationship basically indicates that the Person item relates to the Personal Contacts folder as a member of the folder.

When you define a relationship, you define whether the relationship keeps the target item in existence—a *holding relationship*—or doesn't keep the target item in existence— a *reference relationship*. When you create a holding relationship to a target item, WinFS increments a reference count on the target item. When WinFS deletes a holding relationship it decrements the reference count on the target item. An item no longer exists in the store when its reference count reaches zero. WinFS never alters the reference count of the target when you create or destroy a reference relationship to the target. Therefore, the target item can disappear from the store when its reference count reaches zero and the relationship might refer to a no-longer-existing item.

WinFS defines the *FolderMember* relationship as a holding relationship. Most other relationship classes are reference relationships.

Folder Items

Now that you know about Link items, I can refine my description of Folder items. A Folder is a WinFS item that has a collection of Link items. The target of each Link item in the collection is a member of the folder. The *Folder.Members* property represents this collection of links.

Note this gives a WinFS folder much greater flexibility than traditional file system folders. The members of a folder can be file and nonfile items. Multiple links to a particular item can reside in many folders concurrently. In other words, multiple folders can *contain* the same item.

Other Item Types

Generally, you create other item types in the WinFS store as you did in the previous examples. Each type occasionally has its own special usage pattern. For example, we can have organizations as members of our Personal Contacts folder, so let's create one:

```
Organization cp = FindOrCreateOrganization (ctx, "Main Benefit");
...
Organization FindOrCreateOrganization (ItemContext ctx, string orgName) {
  Organization o =
    Organization.FindOne (ctx, "DisplayName='" + orgName + "'");
  if (o == null) {
    Folder Pcf = UserDataFolder.FindMyPersonalContactsFolder (ctx);

    o = new Organization (ctx);
    o.DisplayName = orgName;

    Folder pcf = UserDataFolder.FindMyPersonalContactsFolder (ctx);

    pcf.AddMember (o, o.DisplayName.ToString ());
    ctx.Update ();
  }
  return o;
}
```

Now let's add an employee to that organization:

```
enum Names { Monica, Rachel, Chandler, Joey, Phoebe, Ross }
...
Person[] Friends = CreateFriends (ctx);
Organization cp = FindOrCreateOrganization (ctx, "Main Benefit");
AddEmployeeToOrganization (ctx, Friends [(int)Names.Rachel],
  cp);
...
```

```
void AddEmployeeToOrganization (ItemContext ctx, Person p, Organization o) {
  EmployeeData ed = new EmployeeData (ctx);

  ed.Name = p.DisplayName;
  ed.Target_Key = p.ItemID_Key;
  o.Employees.Add (ed);
  ctx.Update ();
}
```

Similarly, we can create households in our Personal Contacts folders. Note that a household doesn't imply a family. A household might be a group of roommates. WinFS has additional schema for families, but I'll leave that as an exercise for the reader.

```
CreateHousehold (ctx, Friends [(int) Names.Chandler],
                      Friends [(int) Names.Joey]);
CreateHousehold (ctx, Friends [(int) Names.Monica],
                      Friends [(int) Names.Rachel]);
...
void CreateHousehold (ItemContext ctx, Person p1, Person p2) {
  Household h = new Household (ctx);
  h.DisplayName = p1.GetPrimaryName().GivenName + " and " +
                  p2.GetPrimaryName().GivenName + " household";

  Folder pcf = UserDataFolder.FindMyPersonalContactsFolder (ctx);
  pcf.AddMember (h, h.DisplayName.ToString ());

  // Add first person to the household
  HouseholdMemberData hhmd = new HouseholdMemberData (ctx);
  hhmd.Name = p1.DisplayName;
  hhmd.Target_Key = p1.ItemID_Key;
  h.HouseholdMembers.Add (hhmd);

  // Add second person to the household
  hhmd = new HouseholdMemberData (ctx);
  hhmd.Name = p2.DisplayName;
  hhmd.Target_Key = p2.ItemID_Key;
  h.HouseholdMembers.Add (hhmd);
}
```

The prior example uses one concept I've not yet discussed. Note the use of the *ItemID_Key* property in this line of code:

```
hhmd.Target_Key = p1.ItemID_Key;
```

Basically, the *ItemID_Key* value is another way to reference an item in the WinFS store, so let's look at the ways to find items in the store.

How to Find Items

Of course, it doesn't do much good to place items in a data store if you cannot subsequently find them easily. The *ItemContext* class contains instance methods you can use to retrieve items in a WinFS data store. You specify what type of item to find and any special constraints that the returned items must meet. In addition, each item class—for example, *Person*, *File*, *Folder*, and so forth—also contains static methods that allow you to find items of that particular type.

The *FindAll* method returns one or more items that match the specified criteria. The *ItemContext.FindAll* instance method requires you to specify the type of the items to locate. In addition, you can optionally specify search criteria to narrow the scope of search. For example, the following code finds all the Person items that have a *DisplayName* property whose value begins with "Brent".

```
FindResult res = ctx.FindAll (typeof(Person), "DisplayName='Brent%'");
foreach (Person p in res) {
    // Use the Person item somehow
}
```

Alternatively, I could use the static *FindAll* method of the *Person* class like this:

```
FindResult res = Person.FindAll (ctx, "DisplayName='Brent%'");
foreach (Person p in res) {
    // Use the Person item somehow
}
```

In both of these examples, the *FindAll* method always returns a collection of the items matching the type and specified criteria. This collection might contain no items, but you don't receive a null reference for the *FindResult*. Therefore, always iterate over the collection to obtain the items found.

When you know that only a single item will match the type requested and specified filter criteria, you can use the *FindOne* method. Be careful, however—the *FindOne* method throws an exception when it finds more than one item that matches your request.

```
Person p = Person.FindOne (ctx, "DisplayName='Brent Rector'");
```

The second string parameter is a filter expression that allows you to specify additional constraints the returned items must satisfy. The basic format of the filter expression is a string in the form "*<propertyName> <operator> <propertyValue>*".

WinFS calls the expression an *OPath* expression. The syntax is similar, although not identical, to the *XPath* expression syntax used for identifying items in an XML document. This code fragment returns all File items for files with either a "doc" or a "txt" file extension:

```
FindResult Files = File.FindAll (ctx, "Extension='doc' || Extension='txt'");
```

These expressions can be quite complex. For example, the following statement returns all Person items that represent employees of an employer with the *DisplayName* of "Main Benefit":

```
string pattern = "Source(EmployeeOf).DisplayName='Main Benefit'";
FindResult result = Person.FindAll (ctx, pattern);
```

Here's another one. I want the Person items where the Surname is not "Ranier" and the e-mail addresses don't end with ".edu".

```
string filter = "PersonalNames[Surname!='Ranier'] &&
                !(PersonalEmailAddresses[Address like '%.edu'])");
FindResult result = Person.FindAll (ctx, filter);
```

Identifying a Specific Item

You frequently need to create references to items in the WinFS store. Eventually, you use these references to locate the appropriate item. Earlier in this chapter, I showed you how to use a link to reference an item. Links use a friendly string-based identity for the reference, and this string name must be unique within the link's containing folder. In other words, you need both the folder and one of its contained links to identify the referenced item.

However, you can create multiple links with the same friendly string name as long as you add the links to different folders so that all names within a single folder remain unique. Note that these multiple links with the same friendly text name don't actually have to reference the same target item. They could, but they don't have to.

In such cases, searching for all links with a specific friendly text name (using *FindAll*, for example) will return multiple results. You will then need to examine the source of each link to determine the containing folder, and then determine which link references the desired item.

We need a way to reference any arbitrary item in the store—for example, suppose I want the 3,287th item in the store. Fortunately, you can do exactly this.

Finding an Item by *ItemID_Key* Value

WinFS assigns each newly created item a GUID-based identification number, known as its *ItemID_Key* property. In practice, an *ItemID_Key* value is highly likely to be unique across all WinFS volumes; however, WinFS still treats this identifier as if it's unique only within a volume. You can use this volume unique value to identify any item in a WinFS volume.

```
Item GetItem (ItemContext ctx, SqlBinary itemID_Key) {
  // Convert itemID_Key to a string for use in the OPath filter
  string hexItemID_Key = BitConverter.ToString (itemID_Key.Value);
  hexItemID_Key = "'0x" + hexItemID_Key.Replace ("-", String.Empty) + "'";

  // Build an opath filter expression.
  string query = "ItemID_Key=" + hexItemID_Key;
   return Item.FindOne (ctx, query);
}
```

Common Features

WinFS API provides several features across the entire spectrum of data classes. These features are

- Asynchrony
- Transactions
- Notifications
- Blob/stream support
- Cursoring and paging

Asynchrony

The WinFS API allows you to run queries asynchronously. The WinFS API uses the .NET standard asynchronous programming model patterns.

Transactions

The WinFS store is a transactional store. WinFS, therefore, allows you to make transactional updates to the store using the *BeginTransaction*, *CommitTransaction*, and *AbortTransaction* methods on the *ItemContext* object, as shown in the following example:

```
using (ItemContext ctx = ItemContext.Open()) {
  using (Transaction t = ctx.BeingTransaction()) {
    Person p = Person.FindOne (ctx,
        "PersonalNames[GivenName='Chandler' And SurName='Bing']" );
    Household h = Household.FindOne (ctx,
        "DisplayName = 'Chandler and Joey Household'");
    p.PersonalEAddresses.Add (new TelephoneNumber ("202", "555-1234"));
    p.Save ();
    h.Members.Add (p);
    h.Save ();
    t.Commit ();
  }
}
```

Notifications

The WinFS Notification Service uses the concepts of short-term and long-term subscriptions. A *short-term subscription* lasts until an application cancels the subscription or the application exits. A *long-term subscription* survives application restarts. WinFS API *watchers* are a set of classes that allow applications to be selectively notified of changes in the WinFS store and provide state information that can be persisted by the application to support suspend/resume scenarios.

The *Watcher* class can notify your application of changes to different aspects of WinFS objects, including the following:

- Item changes
- Embedded item changes
- Item extension changes
- Relationship changes

When a watcher raises an event, it sends watcher state data with the event notification. Your application can store this state data for later retrieval. Subsequently, you can use this watcher state data to indicate to WinFS that you want to receive events for all changes that occurred after the state was generated.

The watcher programming model also allows any combination of added, modified, and removed events to be disabled. It can also be configured to raise an initial event that simulates the addition of all existing items, item extensions, relationships, and so on.

The WinFS watcher design is broken down into the classes described in the following table.

Class	Purpose/Description
WatcherOptions	Class for specifying initial scope and granularity options to *StoreWatcher*
StoreWatcher	The quintessential class for watching WinFS items, embedded items, item extensions, and relationships
WatcherState	Opaque object that can be used to initialize a *StoreWatcher*
ChangedEventHandler	Class that defines the event handler to be called by *StoreWatcher*
ChangedEventArgs	Class passed as argument to *ChangedEventHandler*
ItemChangeDetail	Base class that provides granular change details for item events
ItemExtensionChangeDetail	Class derived from *ItemChangeDetail* that provides additional change details specific to item extension events
RelationshipChangeDetail	Class derived from *ItemChangeDetail* that provides additional change details specific to relationship events

You use the *StoreWatcher* class to create a watcher for some item in the WinFS store. The *StoreWatcher* instance will raise events when the specified item changes. You can specify the type of item and hierarchy to watch. By default, a watcher

- Does not raise an initial event to establish the current state
- Watches the item and the hierarchy (including immediate children) for any changes
- Raises add, remove, and modify events on this item or any child in entire hierarchy
- Raises add, remove, and modify events for item extensions on this item or any child in entire hierarchy
- Raises add, remove, and modify events for relationships in which this item or any child in entire hierarchy is the source of the relationship

Because by default a watcher watches for changes in the specified item and its descendants, you might want to specify *WatchItemOnly* as the watcher option. The following example watches for changes only to the located Person item:

```
Person p = Person.FindOne (ctx,
            "PersonalNames[GivenName='Rachel' and Surname='Emerald'");
StoreWatcher w = new StoreWatcher ( p, WatcherOptions.WatchItemOnly );
```

A Folder is just another WinFS item. You watch for changes in a Folder the same way you do for a Person:

```
Folder f = • • •
StoreWatcher w = new StoreWatcher (f, <WatcherOptions>);
```

You can watch for changes in a specified relationship of an item, too:

```
Person p = • • •
StoreWatcher w = new StoreWatcher (p, typeof(HouseholdMember),
                                   <WatcherOptions> );
w.ItemChanged += new ChangedEventHandler (ItemChangedHandler);
w.Enabled = true;

// Change notifications now arrive until we unsubscribe from the event
   …
// Now we unsubscribe from the event
w.ItemChanged -= new ChangedEventHandler (ItemChangedHandler);
w.Dispose ();
…

// The change notification handler
void ItemChangedHandler (object source, ChangedEventArgs args) {
  foreach (ItemChangeDetail detail in args.Details) {
    switch (typeof(detail)) {
      case ItemExtensionChangeDetail:
```

```
              // handle added + modified + removed events for Item Extension
              break;

          case RelationshipChangeDetail:
              // handle added + modified + removed events for Relationship
              break;

          default:
          case ItemChangeDetail:
              // handle added + modified + removed events for Item or Embedded Item
              HandleItemChangeDetail (detail);
              break;
        }
      }
    |

    void HandleItemChangeDetail (ItemChangeDetail detail) {
      switch (detail.ChangeType) {
        case Added:          // handle added event
          break;

        case Modified:       // handle modified event
          break;
        case Removed:         // handle modified event
                  break;
      }
    }
```

Blob and Stream Support

Blob and stream support APIs are still in flux at the time of this writing. Check the documentation for the latest information about how to access blobs and streams in the WinFS store.

Cursoring and Paging

The various *Find* methods in the WinFS classes can return a (potentially) large collection of objects. This collection is the equivalent of a rowset in the database world. Traditional database applications use a *paged cursor* to navigate efficiently within a large rowset. This cursor references a single row (a *thin cursor*) or a set of rows (a *page cursor*). The idea is that applications retrieve one page's worth of rows at a time; they can also pinpoint one row within the page for positioned update and delete. The WinFS API provides similar abstractions to the developer for dealing with large collections.

By default, a find operation provides a read-only, scrollable, dynamic cursor over the returned collection. An application can have a fire hose cursor for maximum performance. A fire hose cursor is a forward-only cursor. The application can retrieve a page of rows at a time, but the next retrieval operation will begin with the subsequent set of rows—it cannot go back and re-retrieve rows. In a sense, rows flow from the store to the application like water from a fire hose—hence the name.

The *CursorType* property in the *FindParameters* class will allow an application to choose between a fire hose and scrollable cursor. For both fire hose and scrollable cursors, the application can set a page size using the *PageSize* property of the *FindParameters* class. By default, the page size is set to 1.

Data Binding

You can use the WinFS data classes as data sources in a data-binding environment. The WinFS classes implement *IDataEntity* (for single objects) and *IDataCollection* (for collections) interfaces. The *IDataEntity* interface provides notifications to the data-binding target of changes to properties in the data source object. The *IDataCollection* interface allows the determination of the base type of an object in a polymorphic collection. It also allows you to retrieve a *System.Windows.Data.CollectionManager*, which navigates through the data entities of the collection and provides a view (for example, sort order or filter) of the collection. I discuss data binding in detail in Chapter 5.

Security

The WinFS security model fundamentally grants a set of *Rights* to a *Principal* on an *Item* in the following ways:

- Security is set at the level of *Items*.

- A set of rights can be granted to a security principle on an *Item*. This set includes: READ, WRITE, DELETE, EXECUTE (for all items), CREATE_CHILD, ADMINISTER, and AUDIT. (Additional rights are grantable on Folder items.)

- Users and applications are the security principles. Application rights supersede user rights. When an application doesn't have permission to delete a contact, a user cannot delete it via the application regardless of the user's permissions.

- Security is set using rules; each rule is a *Grant* and applies to a triplet: (*<ItemSet, PrincipalSet, RightSet>*).

- The rules are themselves stored as *Items*.

Getting Rights on an Item

Each WinFS item class has a method named *GetRightsForCurrentUser*, which returns the set of rights—READ, WRITE, DELETE, and so forth—that the current user has on the specified item. In addition, the method returns the set of methods that WinFS allows the user to execute.

Setting Rights on an Item

WinFS uses a special Item type, *SecurityRule*, to store permissions information on *Items*. Thus, setting and changing rights is no different from manipulating any other *Item* in WinFS. Here's a code example showing how to set rights on a folder item:

```
using (ItemContext ctx = ItemContext.Open("\\localhost\WinFS_C$")) {
  SecurityRule sr = new SecurityRule (ctx);
  sr.Grant = true;
  // set permission on items under folder1 including folder1
  sr.AppliesTo = <folder1's Identity Key>;
  sr.Condition = acl1;    // a DACL
  sr.Save();
}
```

Extending the WinFS API

Every built-in WinFS class contains standard methods such as *Find** and has proper-ties for getting and setting field values. These classes and associated methods form the foundation of WinFS APIs and allow you to learn how to use one class and know, in general, how to use many other WinFS classes. However, while standard behavior is useful, each specific data type needs additional, type-specific behaviors.

Domain Behaviors

In addition to these standard methods, every WinFS type will typically have a set of domain-specific methods unique to that type. (Actually, WinFS documentation often refers to type definitions as *schema*, reflecting the database heritage of WinFS.) WinFS refers to these type-specific methods as *domain behaviors*. For example, here are some domain behaviors in the contacts schema:

- Determining whether an e-mail address is valid
- Given a folder, getting the collection of all members of the folder
- Given an item ID, getting an object representing this item
- Given a person, getting his or her online status
- Creating a new contact or a temporary contact with helper functions

Value-Added Behaviors

Data classes with domain behaviors form a foundation that application developers build on. However, it is neither possible nor desirable for data classes to expose every conceivable behavior related to that data.

You can provide new classes that extend the base functionality offered by the WinFS data classes. You do this by writing a class whose methods take one or more of the

WinFS data classes as parameters. In the following example, the *OutlookMainServices* and *WindowsMessageServices* are hypothetical classes that use the standard WinFS *MailMessage* and *Person* classes:

```
MailMessage m = MailMessage.FindOne (…);
OutlookEMailServices.SendMessage(m);

Person p = Person.FindOne (…);
WindowsMessagerServices wms = new WindowsMessagerServices(p);
wms.MessageReceived += new MessageReceivedHandler (OnMessageReceived);
wms.SendMessage("Hello");
```

You can then register these custom classes with WinFS. The registration data will be associated with the schema metadata WinFS maintains for every installed WinFS type. WinFS stores your schema metadata as WinFS items; therefore, you can update, query, and retrieve it as you would all other WinFS items.

Specifying Constraints

The WinFS data model allows value constraints on types. WinFS evaluates and enforces these constraints when you add items to the store. However, you sometimes want to verify that input data satisfies its constraints without incurring the overhead of a roundtrip to the server. WinFS allows the schema/type author to decide whether the type supports client-side constraint checking. When a type supports client-side validation, the type will have a validate method you can call to verify that an object satisfies the specified constraints. Note that regardless of whether the developer calls the *Validate* method, WinFS still checks *class* the constraints at the store.

Using the WinFS API and SQL

The WinFS API enables a developer to access the WinFS store by using familiar common language runtime (CLR) concepts. Throughout this chapter, I used the following coding pattern for WinFS access:

1. Bind to an *ItemContext.*
2. Find the desired items.
3. Update the items.
4. Save all changes back to the store.

Step 2 is essentially a query to the store. The WinFS API uses a filter expression syntax based on *OPath* for specifying these queries. In many cases, using filter expressions should be sufficient for most tasks. However, there will be cases where the developer will want to use the full power and flexibility of SQL.

The following capabilities are present in SQL, but they are not available when using a filter expression:

- Aggregation (*Group By, Having, Rollup*)

- Projection (including calculated select expressions, distinct, *IdentityCol, RowGuidCol*)

- For XML

- Union

- Option

- Right/full/cross join

- Nested selects

- Join to non-WinFS table

It is thus essential that a WinFS developer be able to seamlessly transition between the SQLClient API and the WinFS API, using one or the other in various places in the code.

Aggregate and Group with SQL, and Then Use WinFS API

A small-business owner, Joe, wants to determine who his top 10 customers are and send gift baskets to them. Assume that Customer is a schematized item type. This means that an ISV has provided a schema for the Customer type to WinFS, and therefore, it also means that a WinFS store can now contain Customer items. A Customer item has a holding link to a schematized Order Item type. Order Item has an embedded collection of Line Orders, as follows:

```
1.  using (ItemContext ctx = ItemContext.Open()) {
2.
3.    SqlCommand cmd = ctx.CreateSqlCommand();
4.    cmd.CommandText =
5.     "select object(c) from Customers c inner join (" +
6.      "select top 10 C.ItemId, sum(p.price) " +
7.      "from Customers C" +
8.      "inner join Links L on L.SourceId = C.ItemId" +
9.     "inner join Orders O on L.TargetId = O.ItemId" +
10.     "cross join unnest(O.LineOrders) " +
11.     "group by C.ItemId" +
12.     "order by sum(p.price)) t ON c.ItemId = t.ItemId";
13.
14.   SqlDataReader rdr = cmd.ExecuteReader();
15.
16.   GiftBasketOrder gbOrder = new GiftBasketOrder(Ö);
17.
18.   while (rdr.Read()) {
19.    Customer c = new Customer((CustomerData) rdr.GetValue(0));
20.    // add the customer to gbOrder's recipient collection
```

```
21.    gbOrder.Recipients.Add(c);
22.  }
23.
24.    // send the order. The ISV's GiftBasketOrder can easily pull out
25.    // customer info such as shipping address from the Customer object
26.    gbOrder.Send();
27.  }
```

In line 1 of this example, I open a context for the root of the system volume. In line 3, I create a SQL command object that I subsequently use to execute a SQL query against the WinFS store. This command object reuses the connection used by the item context. Lines 4 through 12 construct the query, and line 14 executes the query. The query returns the top 10 customers in the following manner: the SELECT statement in lines 6 through 12 generates a grouped table containing the total value of each customer's orders; the ORDER BY clause on line 12, combined with the TOP 10 modifier in line 6, selects only the top 10 customers in this grouped table.

The *GiftBasketOrder* class is a custom class that makes use of the WinFS API *Customer* object. I create an instance of *GiftBasketOrder* on line 16.

Line 19 uses the *SQLDataReader* to read the first column of the returned rowset and casts it to a *CustomerData* object.

When you define a new type in WinFS (known as creating a new schema), you are actually defining two types: your managed class and the WinFS store's persistent format of the class. WinFS always adds the *Data* suffix to the name of your class to create the name of the store's type. Therefore, for example, when you define a new Customer type that resides in the WinFS store, WinFS creates the parallel *CustomerData* WinFS User Defined Type (UDT).

The first column of the rowset contains the store's *CustomerData* object. I pass this object to the constructor of the *Customer* class, and the constructor initializes the new object from the *CustomerData* object. This example is typical of using store UDTs to construct WinFS API objects.

Line 24 adds the customer to the *Recipients* collection of the *GiftBasketOrder*.

Finally, I use the *Send* method on gbOrder to "send" this order.

Navigate in API, and Then Aggregate in SQL

Assume that you want to find the average salary (over a 10-year period) for the CEO of each company in my portfolio. Use the following assumptions:

- I have a folder named Companies In My Portfolio, which contains items of type Organization.

■ *EmployeeData* is a link-based relationship, and it has a *YearlyEmploymentHistory* that has the year and the salary for that year.

```
1. using (ItemContext ctx = ItemContext.Open(@"Companies In My Portfolio")) {
2.
3.   SqlCommand cmd = ctx.CreateCommand();
4.   cmd.CommandText =
5.    "select avg( Salary ) from Links l cross apply " +
6.    "( select Salary from unnest( convert(" +
7.    "EmployeeData,l.LinkCol)::YearlyEmploymentHistory )" +
8.    "where Year >= '1993' ) where l.LinkID = @LinkID";
9.
10. SqlParameter param = new SqlParameter ("@LinkID", SqlDbType.BigInt);
11. cmd.Parameters.Add (param);
12.
13. Folder f = Folder.FindByPath (ctx, ".");
14.
15. FindResult orgs = f.GetMembersOfType (typeof(Organization));
16. foreach (Organization o in orgs) {
17.   EmployeeData ed = EmployeeData.FindEmployeeInRole (o,
18.            Organization.Categories.CeoRole);
19.   param.Value = ed.Link.LinkID;
20.   SqlDataReader rdr = cmd.ExecuteReader ();
21.   rdr.Read ();
22.   Console.WriteLine ("{0} ${1}",
23.    ((Person)ed.Target).PersonalNames[0].FullName, rdr.GetFloat(0) );
24.   rdr.Close ();
25. }
26. }
```

Line 1 opens a context for the Companies In My Portfolio WinFS share. Lines 3 through 11 create a parameterized SQL query that I can use in the context of the folder. This query returns the average salary for a given employee (represented by the *@LinkID* parameter). Lines 10 and 11 specify that *@LinkID* is a parameter of type *BigInt*. I execute this query later in the example, on line 20.

Line 13 gets a *Folder* object that represents the folder indicated by the share that I specified when creating the context. Lines 15 and 16 set up the loop for going through the collection of *Organization* objects in this folder.

For each organization, line 17 gets the *EmployeeData* object for the CEO.

Line 19 prepares for the query and sets the value of the parameter to the appropriate LinkID, and then line 20 executes the parameterized SELECT.

Line 21 reads the next and only row from the query result, and lines 22 and 23 print the name of the CEO and the 10-year average salary.

Summary

The WinFS data store provides a far richer data storage model than traditional file systems. Because it supports data, behavior, and relations, it's difficult to categorize WinFS as a file system, a relational database, or an object database. It's a bit of all those technologies in one product. WinFS provides a common definition of ubiquitous information that is globally visible and available to all applications running on Longhorn. Applications can leverage the query, retrieval, transactional update, and filtering capabilities of WinFS; therefore, the developer spends less time developing data access and storage code and more time working on unique application functionality.

Index

A

access, Internet, generic vs. dedicated browsers, 106
Access (AccessDataSource) type, 60
AccessDataSource control class, 60
accessing MapPoint services, 123
Add (HandleCollector) method, 23
adding
  directions to Smartphone, 128–129
  features to Smartphone applications, 126–132
  GPS location to Pocket PCs, 109
  panning to Smartphone, 127
  scrolling to Smartphone, 126
  zooming to Smartphone, 127
AddMemoryPressure method, 14
  demonstrating, 19–21
  object calling, 20
Address property, 151
administration
  ASP.NET version 2, 56–58
  creating new user accounts, 56–57
administrative control, WSE (Web Services Enhancements), 96–97
administrative objects, 56, 58
administrative tools
  ASP.NET version 2, 36
  specifying roles, 54
administrators, problems with ASP.NET version 1, 32
Algorithm (EncryptionMethod) attribute, 101
algorithms, symmetric and asymmetric combined, 99
anonymous personalization, 60
anonymous users, defined, 46
Any object (ObjectDataSource) type, 60
APIs, ClickOnce deployment, 30
App.config file, 79
applications
  maps, 121–132
  programming encryption, 98–103
  Smartphones, adding features, 126–132
  time display, 116–121
  Visual Studio 2003, 117–121

ApplicationUpdateService class, 30
architecture, solution. *See* solution architecture
ArrayList without generics holding objects of any class, 16
arrays, PushPin object, 124
ASP.NET, 31–65
  administration, version 2, 56–58
  administrative tools, version 2, 36
  capabilities, version 2, 35–39
  configuration database, 35–36
  content pages, 37
  content placeholders, 37
  data access, 60–61
  master pages, 37
  navigating master site documents, 40–45
  personalization, 38
  Personalization, 58–60
  prefabricated forms authentication, 35
  prefabrication, infrastructural code, 31
  security, version 2, 45–55
  skins, 38, 61–65
  themes, 38, 61–65
  Web Parts, 39
  Whidbey Alpha version, 35
ASP.NET version 1. *See also* *Introducing Microsoft .NET, Third Edition*
  administration limitations, 32
  configuring Web page layouts for particular users, 34
  developing with IIS required, 34
  overview, 31–34
  password management features, lack of, 32
  personalizing Web visits, 33
  prefabrication, Web design elements, 33–34
  user management features, lack of, 32
ASP.NET version 2. *See* ASP.NET
assigning privileges to roles, 53–55
asymmetric algorithms, 99
asymmetric and symmetric algorithms, combined, 99
attacks, man-in-the-middle, 93
attributes. *See individual attributes*

authentication, 45–53
  forms, 35, 47–53
  credentials, passing as parameters to function calls, 70
  password, complex example, 85–93
  providing security architecture, 69–71
  storing hashed passwords, 92
  UsernameToken object, 87
  Windows-based, described, 46
authorization, 53–55
  assigning privileges to roles, 53–55
  providing rules, 53–55
  roles, 55
automatic memory management, 10–11
automatically checking for updates, ClickOnce deployment, 25–30

B

BasicBlue theme, skins, 62
bilingual data entry system, 108
binding process, WinFS, 164
boxing, defined, 17
browsers, generic vs. dedicated, 106

C

calculating distance of point to location, 143
calling AddMemoryPressure and RemoveMemoryPressure methods, 20
calling for directions, MapPoint Route service, 128
capabilities, ASP.NET version 2, 35–39
catching expired timestamp with tracing, 84
categories, WinFS service, defined, 162
category-based organization, 163
cell phone location capabilities, MapPoint Location Server, 116
cell phones, intelligent. *See* Smartphones

David S. Platt

David S. Platt teaches *Programming .NET* at Harvard University and at companies all over the world. He was named a Software Legend by Microsoft in 2002. He is the author of eight previous books on programming. His most recent title, *Introducing Microsoft .NET, Third Edition,* from Microsoft Press is currently outselling Tom Clancy's *Every Man a Tiger* on Amazon.com, which tells you what kind of geeks buy their books there. "He's the only guy I know that can actually make an article on COM's apartment threading model funny," said one reader.

Dave holds the Master of Engineering degree from Dartmouth College. He did his undergraduate work at Colgate University. When he finishes working, he spends his free time working some more. He wonders whether he should tape down two of his daughter's fingers so she learns how to count in octal. He lives in Ipswich, Massachusetts.

Nickname: The Mad Professor

Favorite Web Site: *http://www.radiomargaritaville.com*

Comment most frequently elicited from children at adjoining breakfast restaurant tables before he's had his morning coffee: "Mommy, what's wrong with that man?"

Learn how to *build dynamic, scalable Web applications* with ASP.NET!

Designing Microsoft® ASP.NET Applications
ISBN 0-7356-1348-6

Get expert guidance on how to use the powerful new functionality of ASP.NET! ASP.NET, the next generation of Active Server Pages, provides a new programming model based on the Microsoft .NET Framework for writing Web applications. Learn about ASP.NET development—with reusable code samples in languages such as Microsoft Visual Basic® .NET and Microsoft Visual C#™—in DESIGNING MICROSOFT ASP.NET APPLICATIONS. This book provides an in-depth look at how to create ASP.NET applications and how they work under the covers. You'll learn how to create Web Forms and reusable components, and how to develop XML Web services. You'll also learn how to create database-enabled ASP.NET applications that use XML (Extensible Markup Language) and ADO.NET (the next generation of Microsoft ActiveX® Data Objects).

Building Web Solutions with ASP.NET and ADO.NET
ISBN 0-7356-1578-0

Take your Web programming skills to the next level. Most Web applications follow a simple "3F" pattern: fetch, format, and forward to the browser. With this in-depth guide, you'll take your ASP.NET and ADO.NET skills to the next level and learn key techniques to develop more functional Web applications. Discover how to build applications for ad hoc and effective Web reporting, applications that work disconnected from the data source and use XML to communicate with non-.NET systems, and general-purpose applications that take advantage of the data abstraction of ADO.NET. Along the way, you'll learn how to take advantage of code reusability, user controls, code-behind, custom Web controls, and other timesaving techniques employed by ASP.NET experts.

Microsoft ASP.NET Step by Step
ISBN 0-7356-1287-0

Master ASP.NET with the proven Microsoft STEP BY STEP learning method. Get a solid handle on this revolutionary new programming framework and its underlying technologies with this accessible, modular primer. You'll quickly learn how to put together the basic building blocks to get working in ASP.NET and find examples drawn from the real-world challenges that both beginning and experienced developers face every day. Easy-to-grasp instructions help you understand fundamental tools and technologies such as the common language runtime, Web Forms, XML Web services, and the Microsoft .NET Framework. Throughout the book, you'll find insightful tips about best practices to follow while using ASP.NET to create scalable, high-performance Web applications.

Microsoft Press has many other titles to help you put development tools and technologies to work. To learn more about the full line of Microsoft Press® products for developers, please visit:

microsoft.com/mspress/developer

Inside information about *Microsoft .NET*

Applied Microsoft® .NET Framework Programming
ISBN 0-7356-1422-9

The expert guidance you need to succeed in .NET Framework development. The Microsoft .NET Framework allows developers to quickly build robust, secure Microsoft ASP.NET Web Forms and XML Web service applications, Windows® Forms applications, tools, and types. Find out all about its common language runtime and learn how to leverage its power to build, package, and deploy any kind of application or component. This book by renowned programming author Jeffrey Richter is ideal for anyone who understands object-oriented programming concepts such as data abstraction, inheritance, and polymorphism. The book carefully explains the extensible type system of the .NET Framework, examines how the runtime manages the behavior of types, and explores how an application manipulates types. While focusing on C#, it presents concepts applicable to all programming languages that target the .NET Framework.

Programming Microsoft .NET
ISBN 0-7356-1376-1

Learn how to develop robust, Web-enabled and Microsoft Windows–based applications by taking advantage of C# and the Microsoft .NET Framework. The Microsoft .NET initiative builds on industry standards to make interoperable software services available anywhere, on any device, over the Internet. Behind the initiative is the Microsoft .NET Framework, which combines a managed run-time environment with one of the richest class libraries ever invented to make building and deploying Web-enabled applications easier than ever. Find out how to leverage the full power of the .NET Framework with this definitive, one-stop resource, written by a leading authority in his trademark easy-to-follow, conversational style. You'll learn about the key programming models embodied in the .NET Framework, including Windows Forms, Web Forms, and XML Web services. And, you'll benefit from a wealth of how-to examples, code samples, and complete working programs in C#.

Microsoft .NET Compact Framework
ISBN 0-7356-1725-2

Build killer applications for handheld devices with the .NET Compact Framework! The Microsoft .NET Compact Framework brings the power of the .NET Framework to handheld devices such as Pocket PCs and smart phones. Learn exactly how to build killer applications—and how to solve typical problems—in developing for resource-constrained devices with this book. You'll find specifics on how to develop GUI elements with Windows Forms, access and store data with ADO.NET and integrate it across the enterprise with XML Web services, work with Microsoft SQL Server™ CE, develop applications that work across wireless networks, and more. You even get code samples plus a quick reference to differences between the .NET Compact Framework and the full .NET Framework.

To learn more about the full line of Microsoft Press® products for developers, please visit:

microsoft.com/mspress/developer